This Book Belongs To

....

The «One Color Arts» book is the unique coloring book you've ever tried! While coloring closed elements of different sizes with just One Color of pen, pencil or marker, you get 30 amazing art-works with fantastic birds and beautiful flowers. You can also use more than one color for a surprising result!

This therapy is a great alternative to a mediation and at the same time, you train your brain: coloring stimulates those parts of a brain which increase concentration and attention.

This is the perfect book to take on the go as it is of the lettersize format and lightweight.

Relax with just One Color!

Copyright © 2019 by SunLife Drawing
All rights reserved
No part of this publication may be reproduced, distributed, or transmitted in any form or by any means, including photocopying, recording, or other electronic or mechanical methods, without the prior written permission of the author, except in the case of brief quotations embodied in critical reviews and certain other noncommercial uses permitted by copyright law.
mail@sunlifedrawing.com

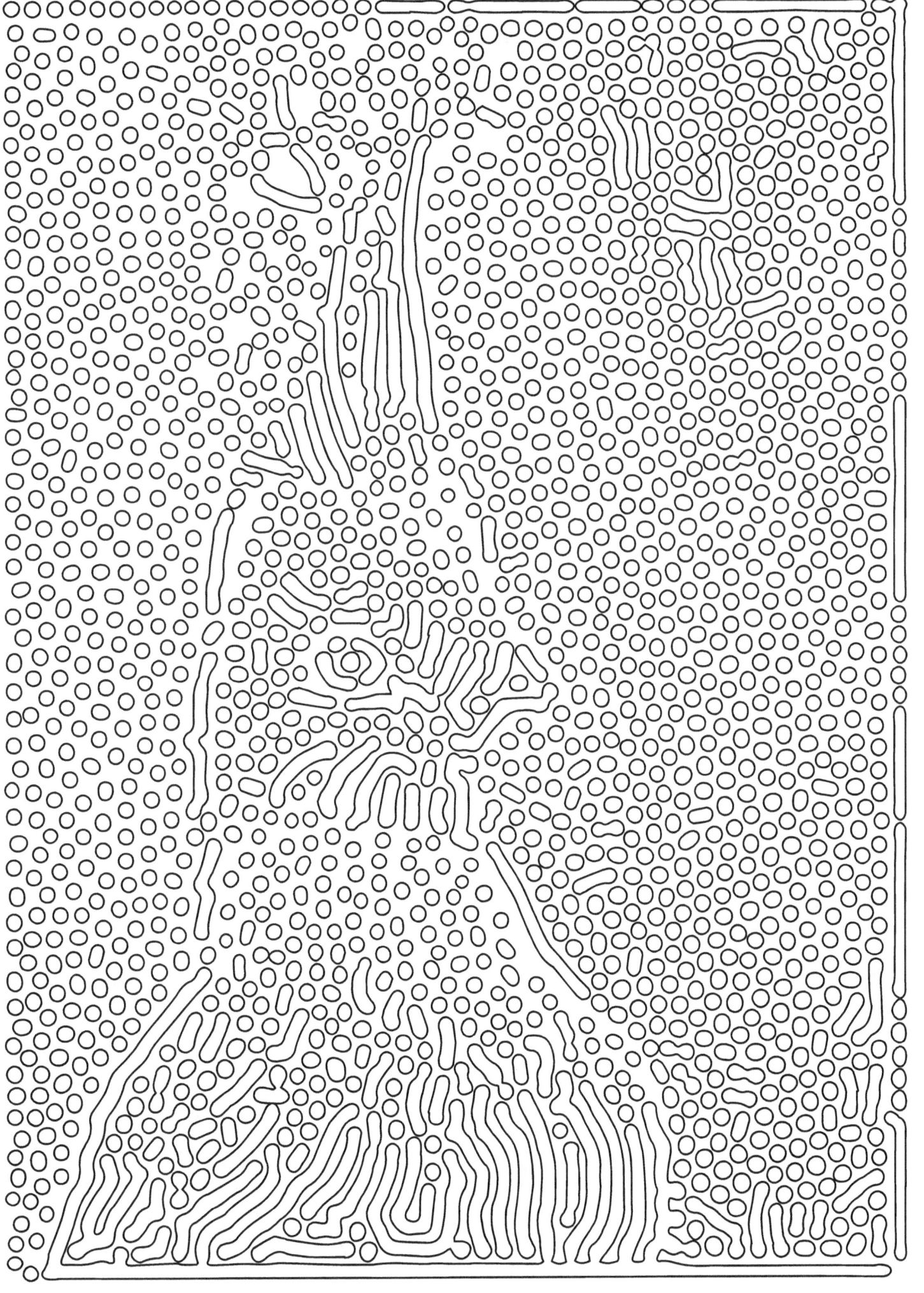

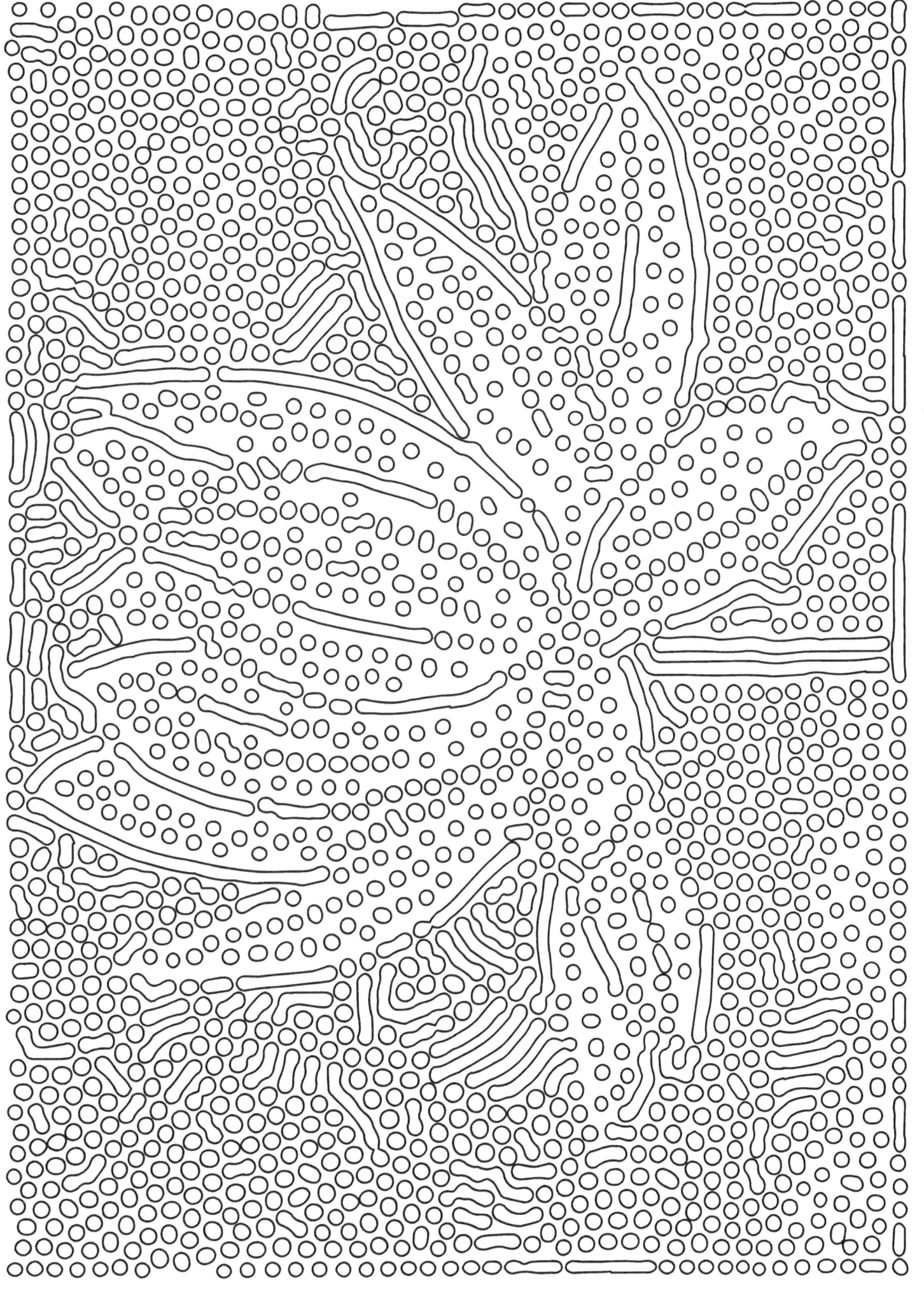

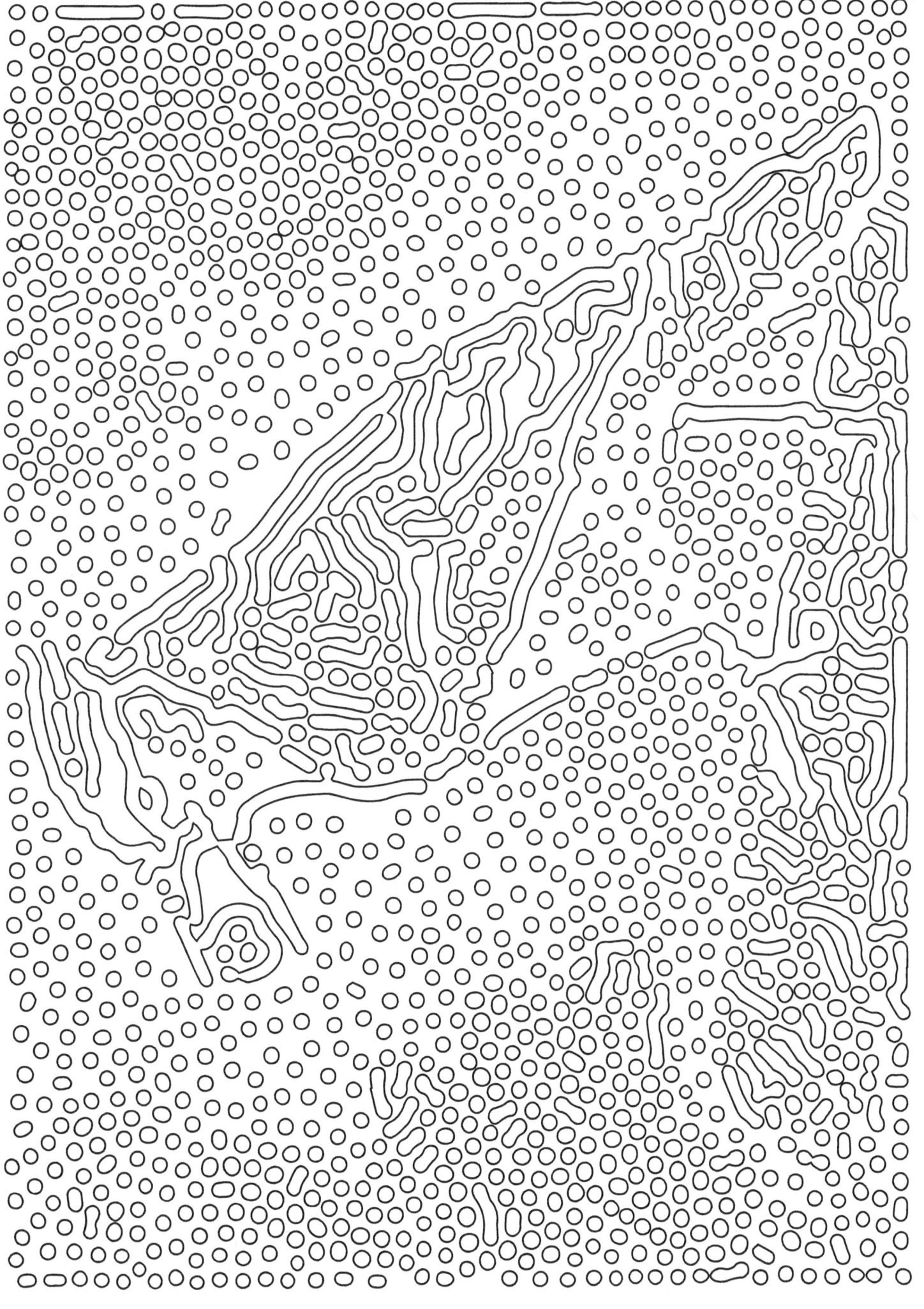

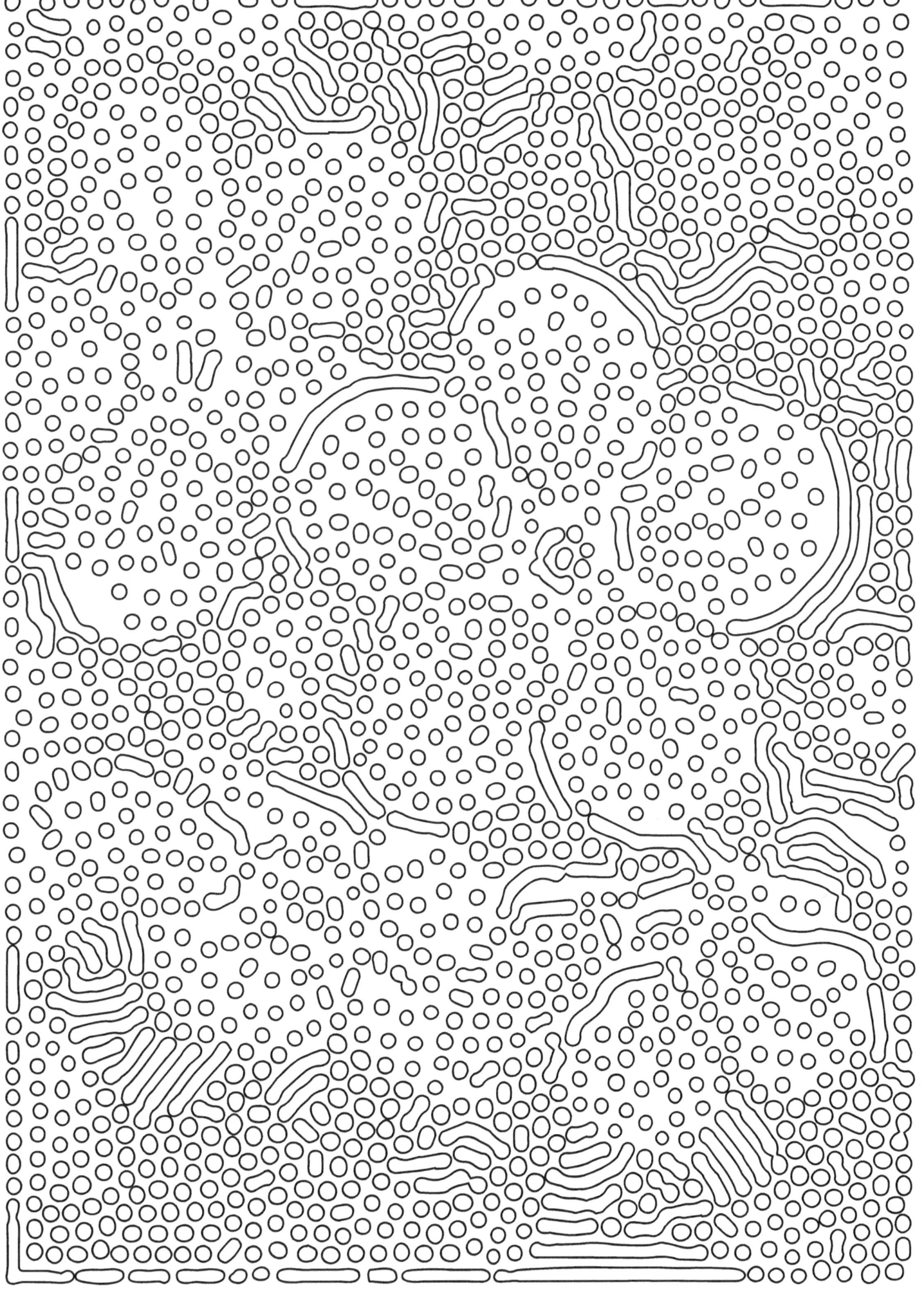

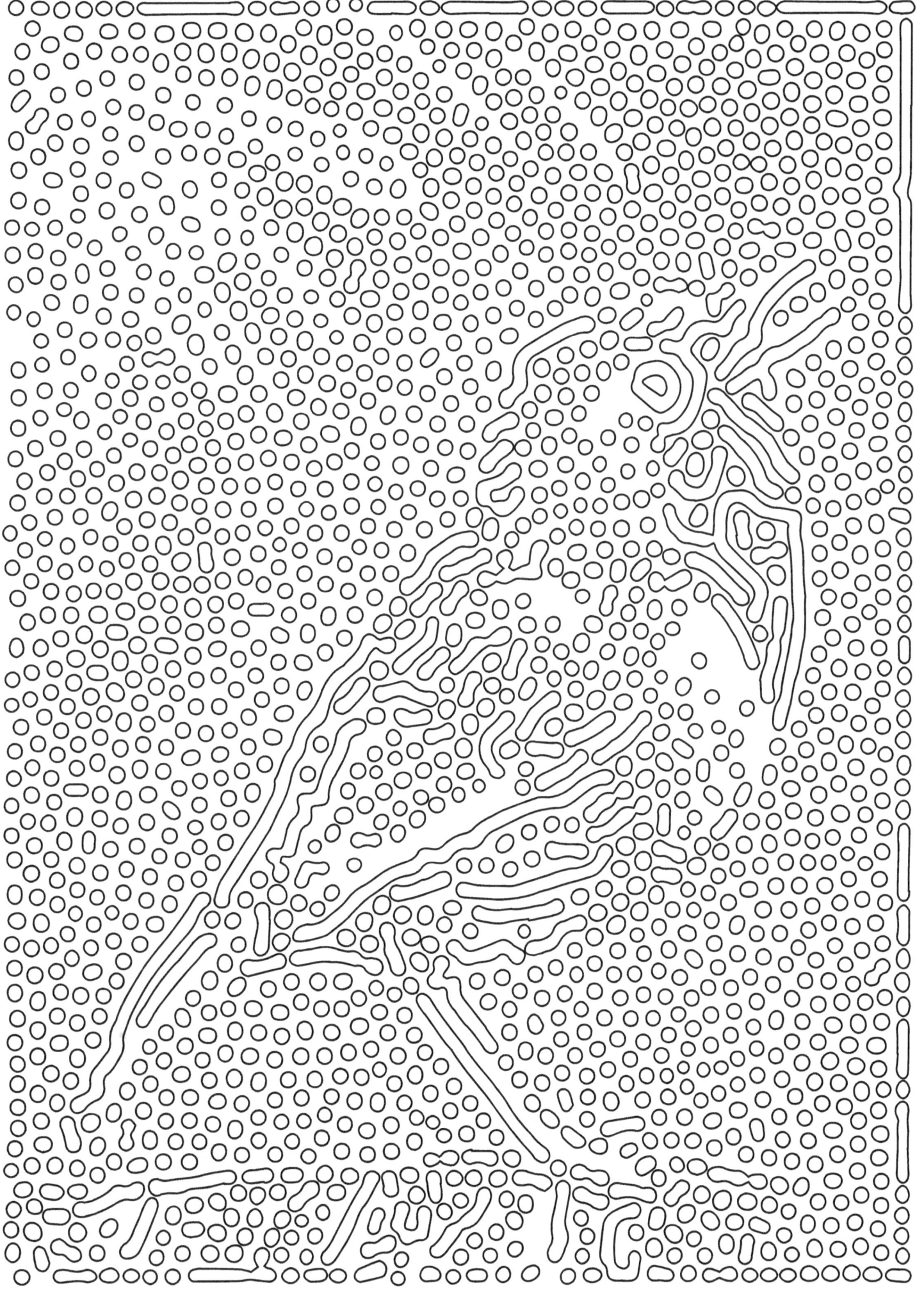

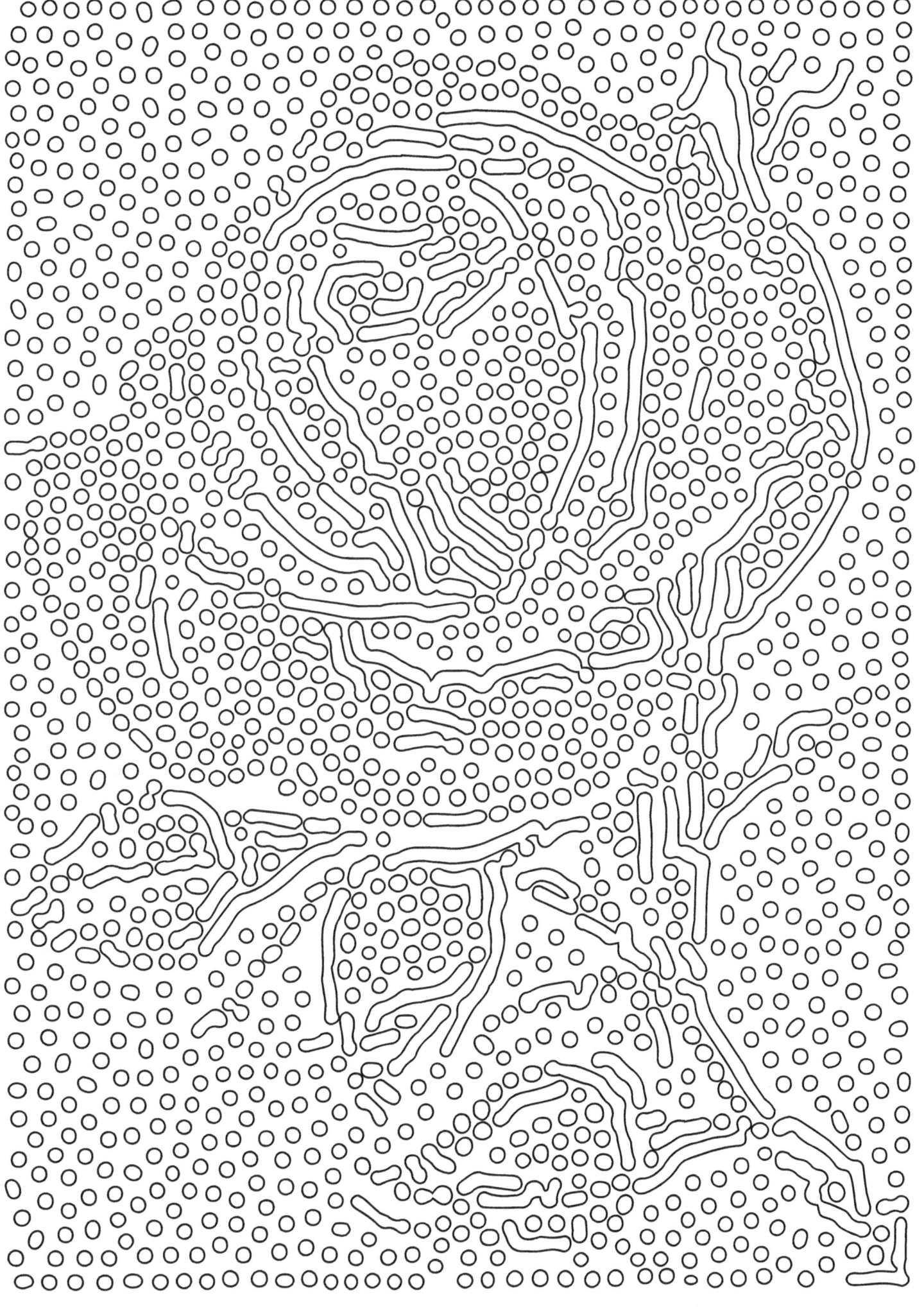

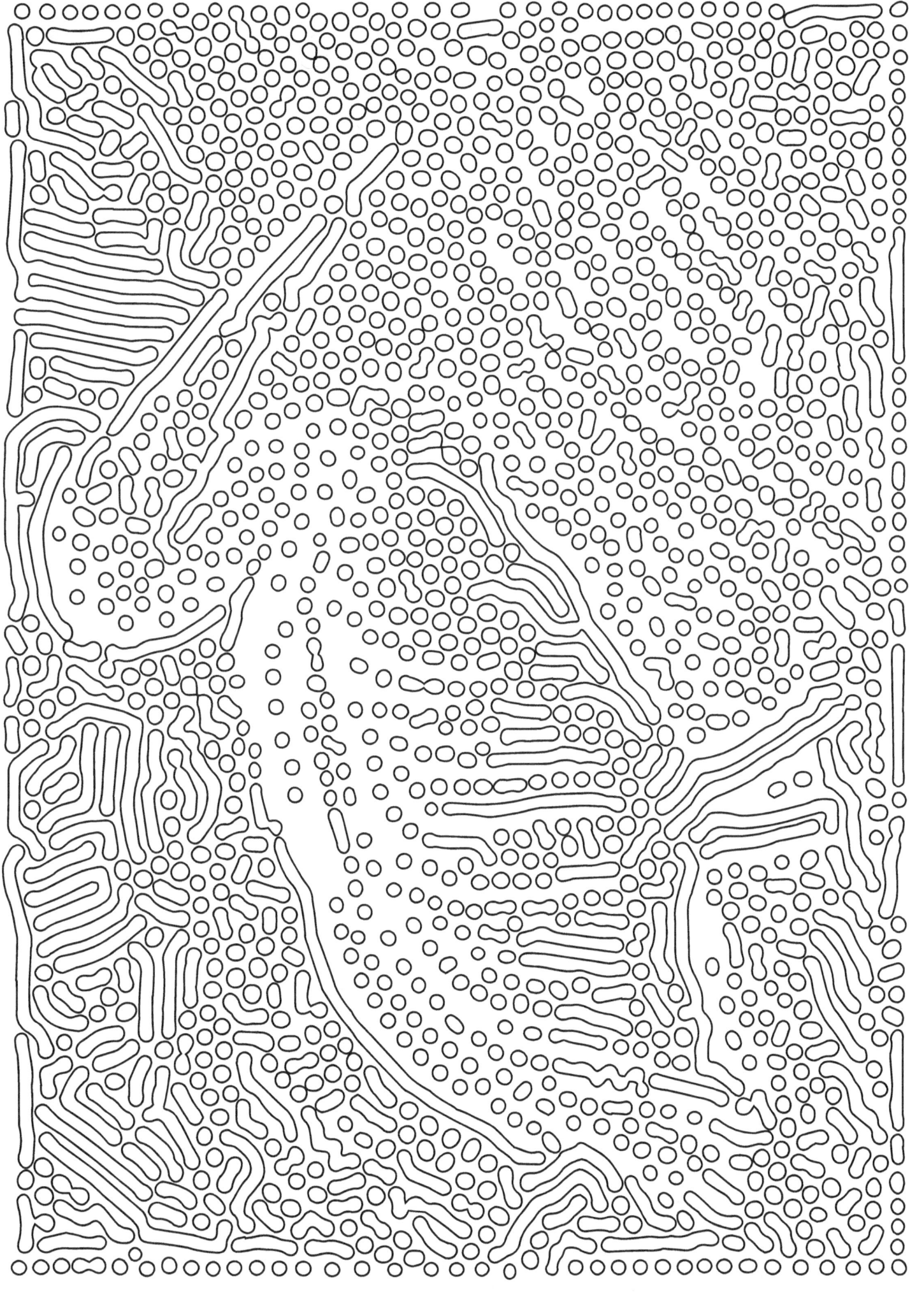

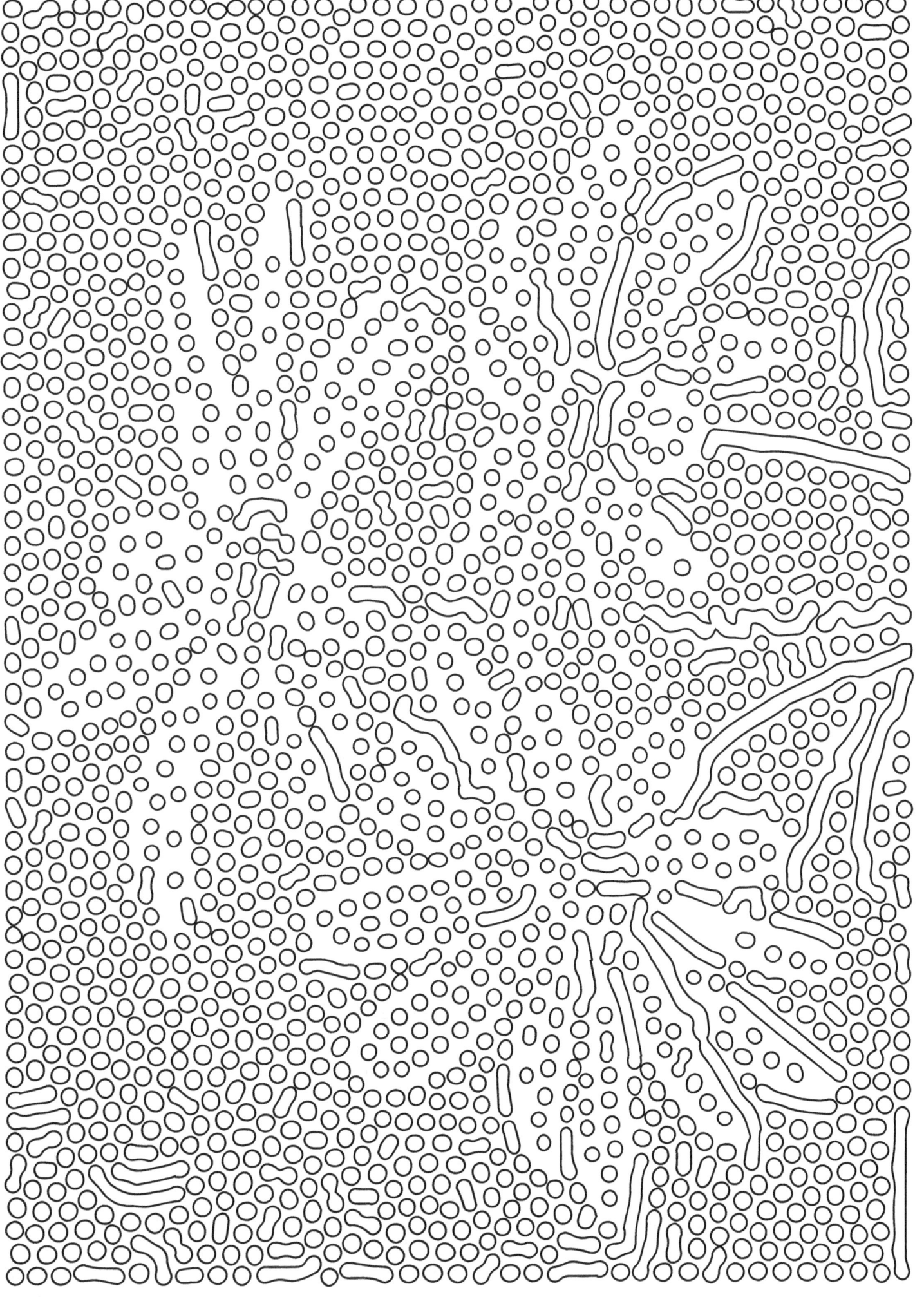

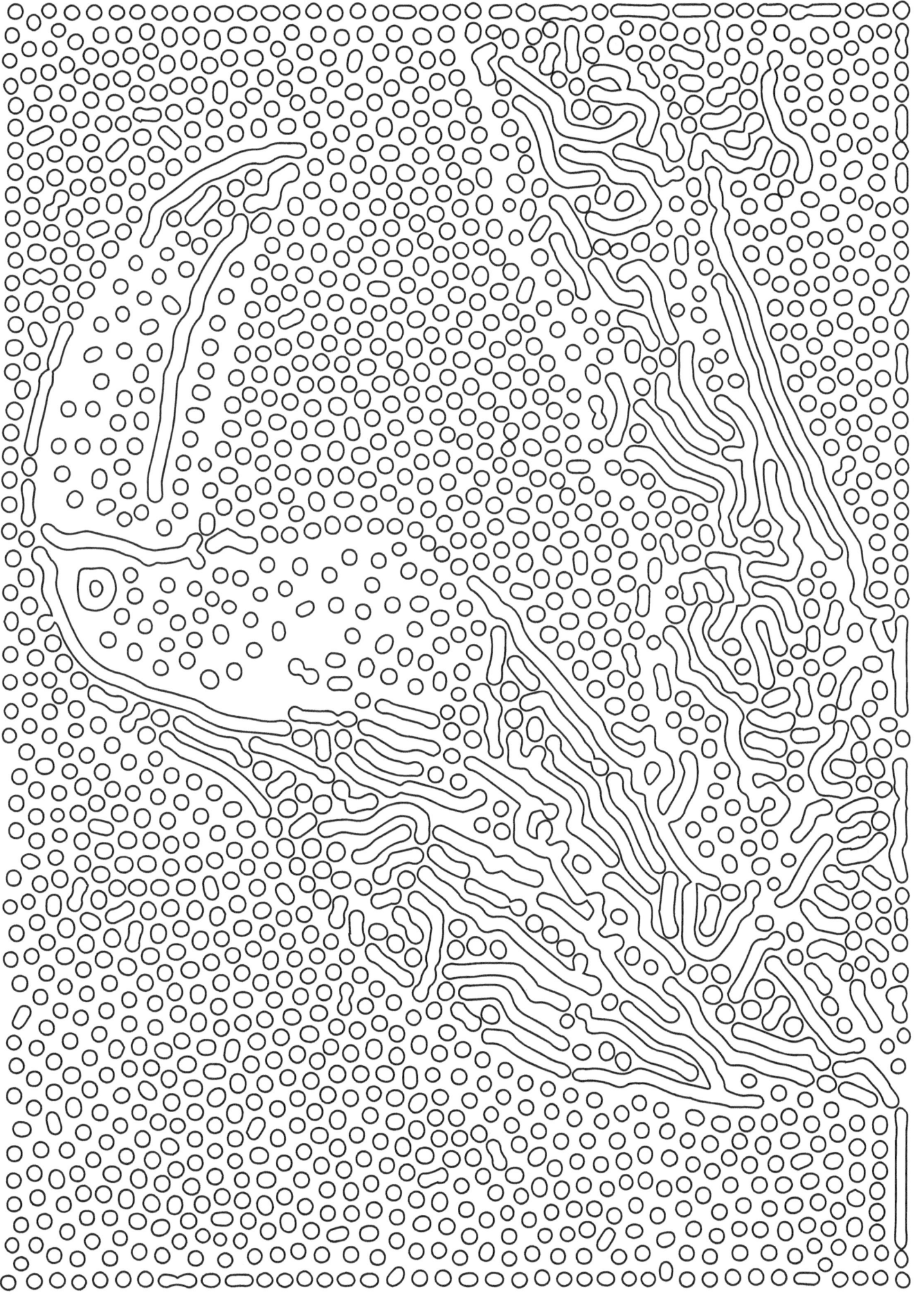

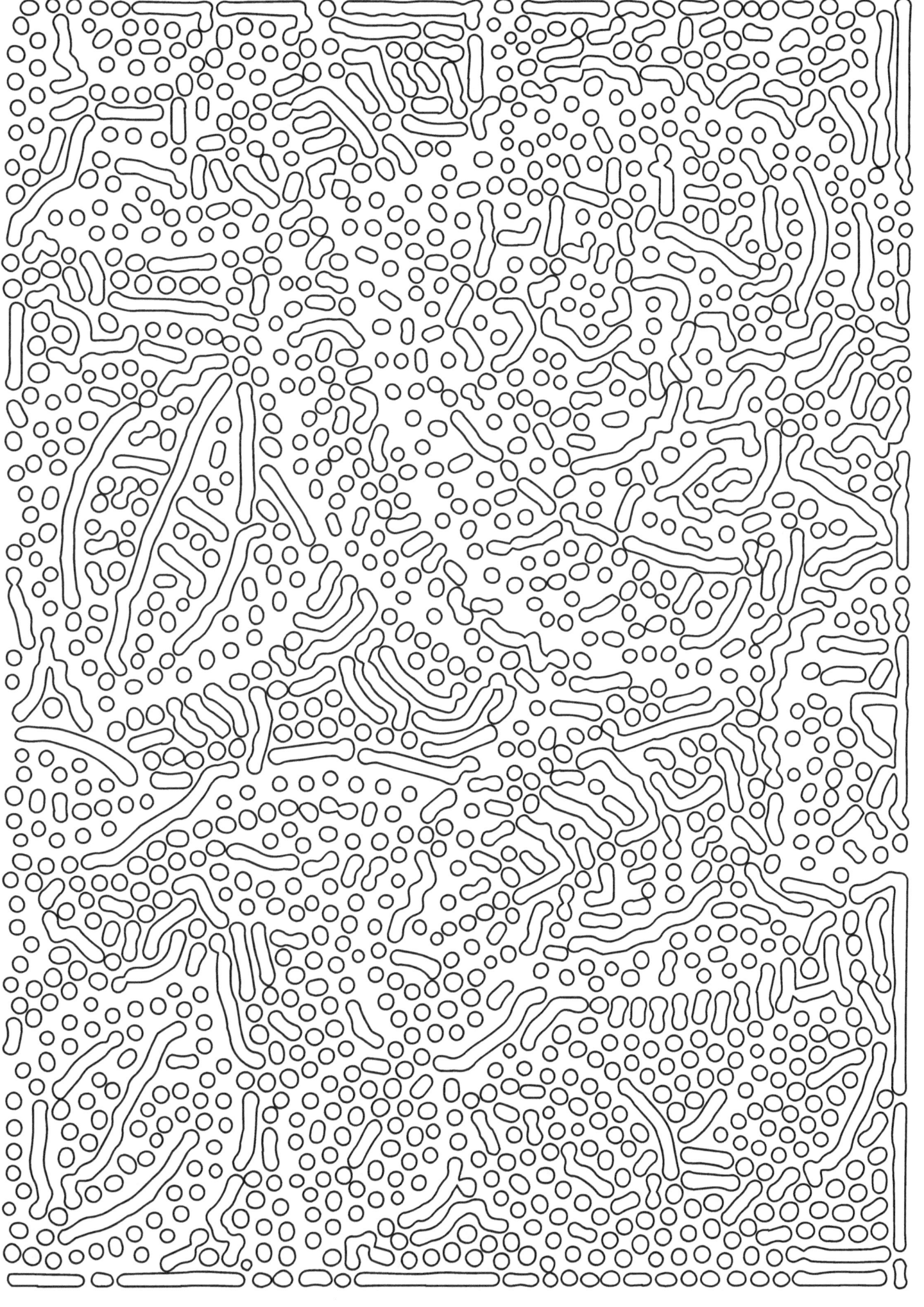

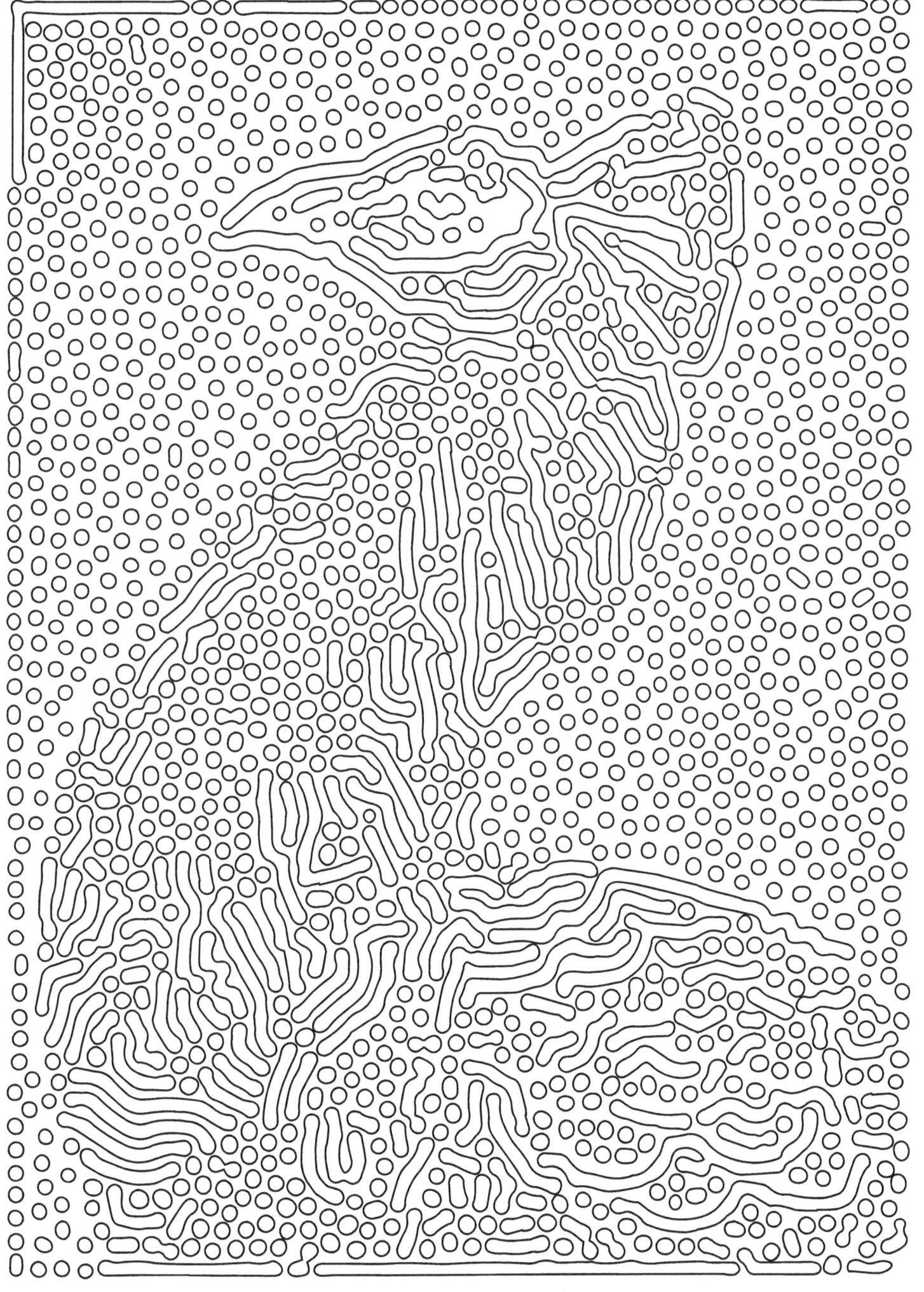

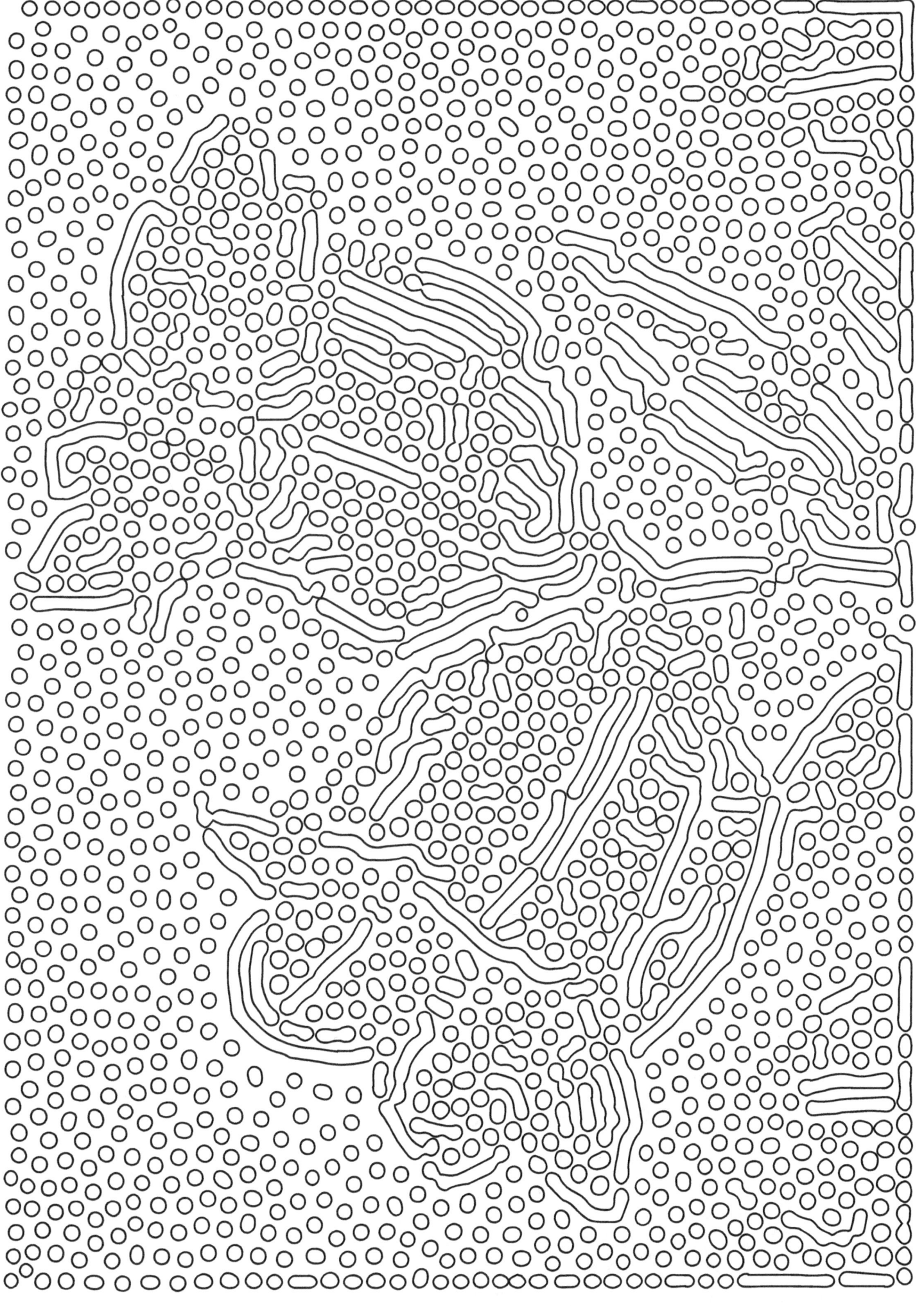

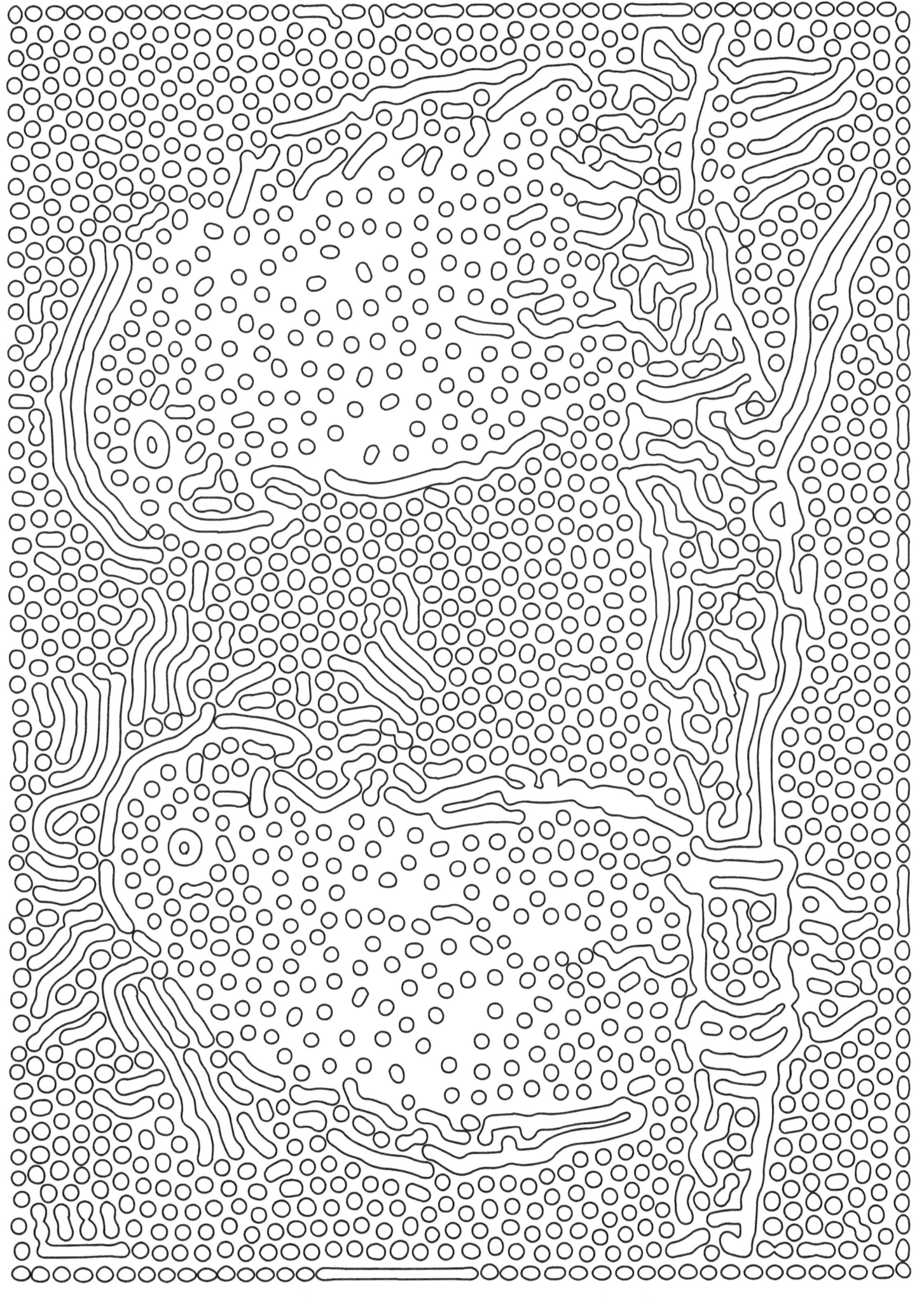

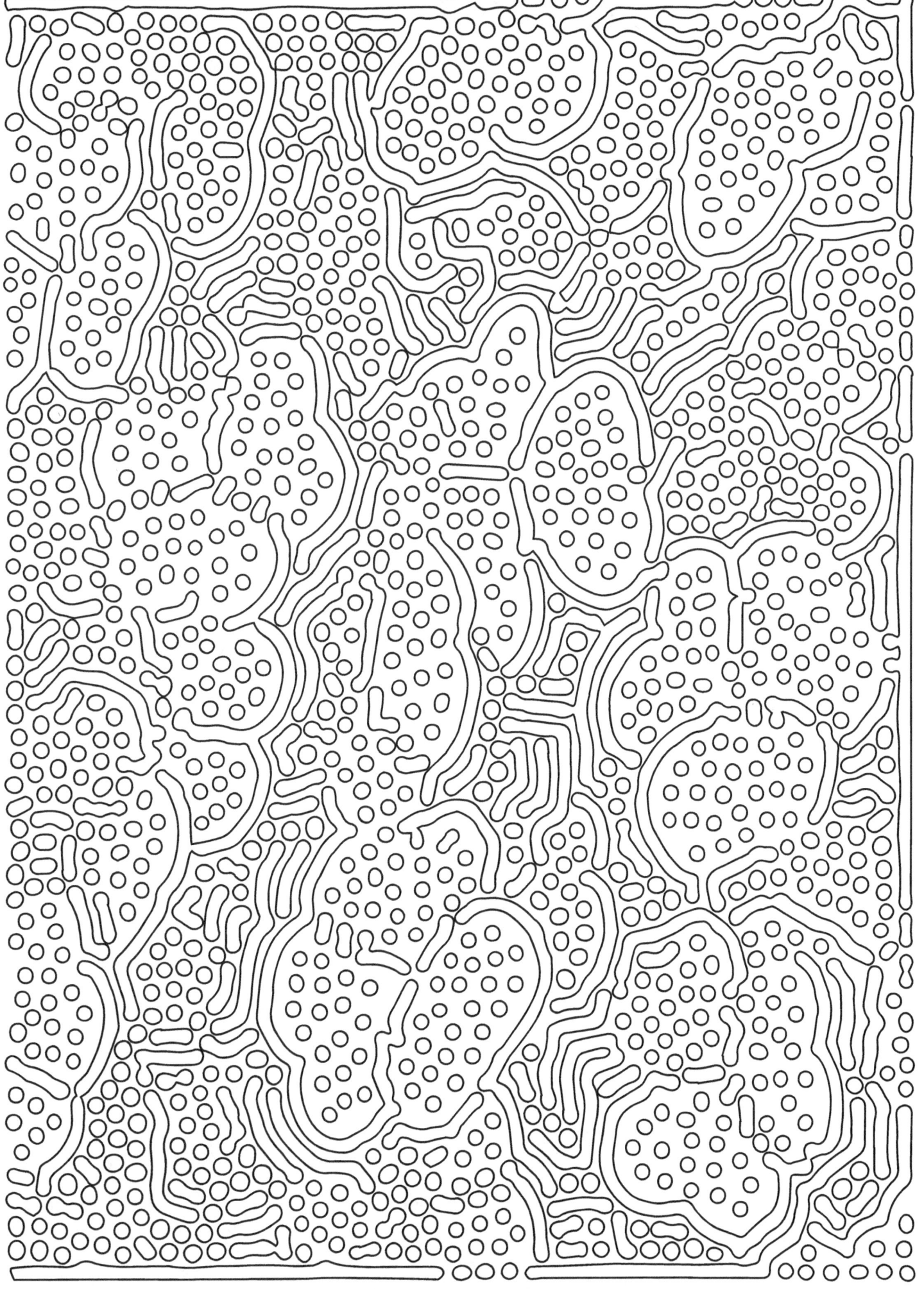

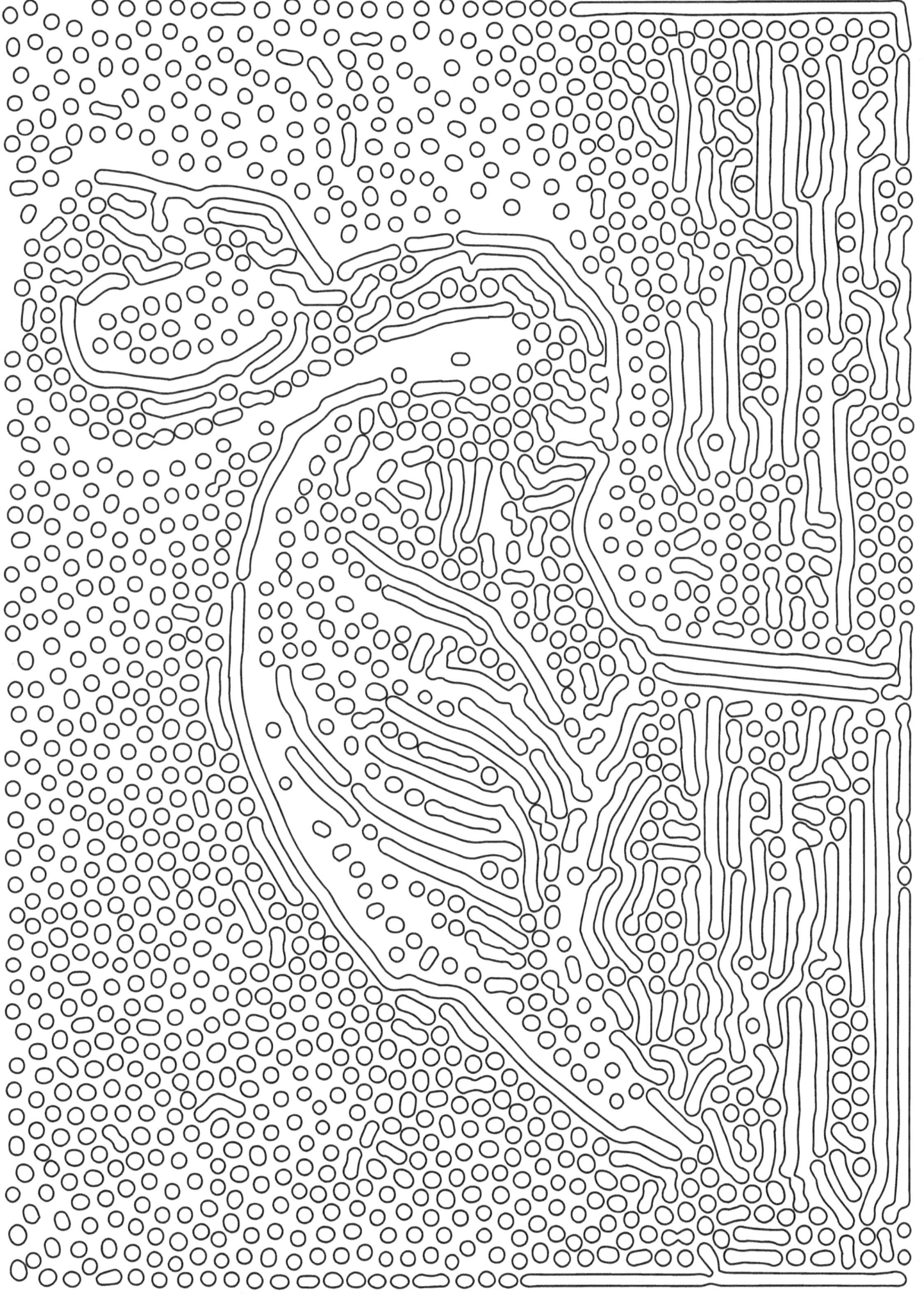

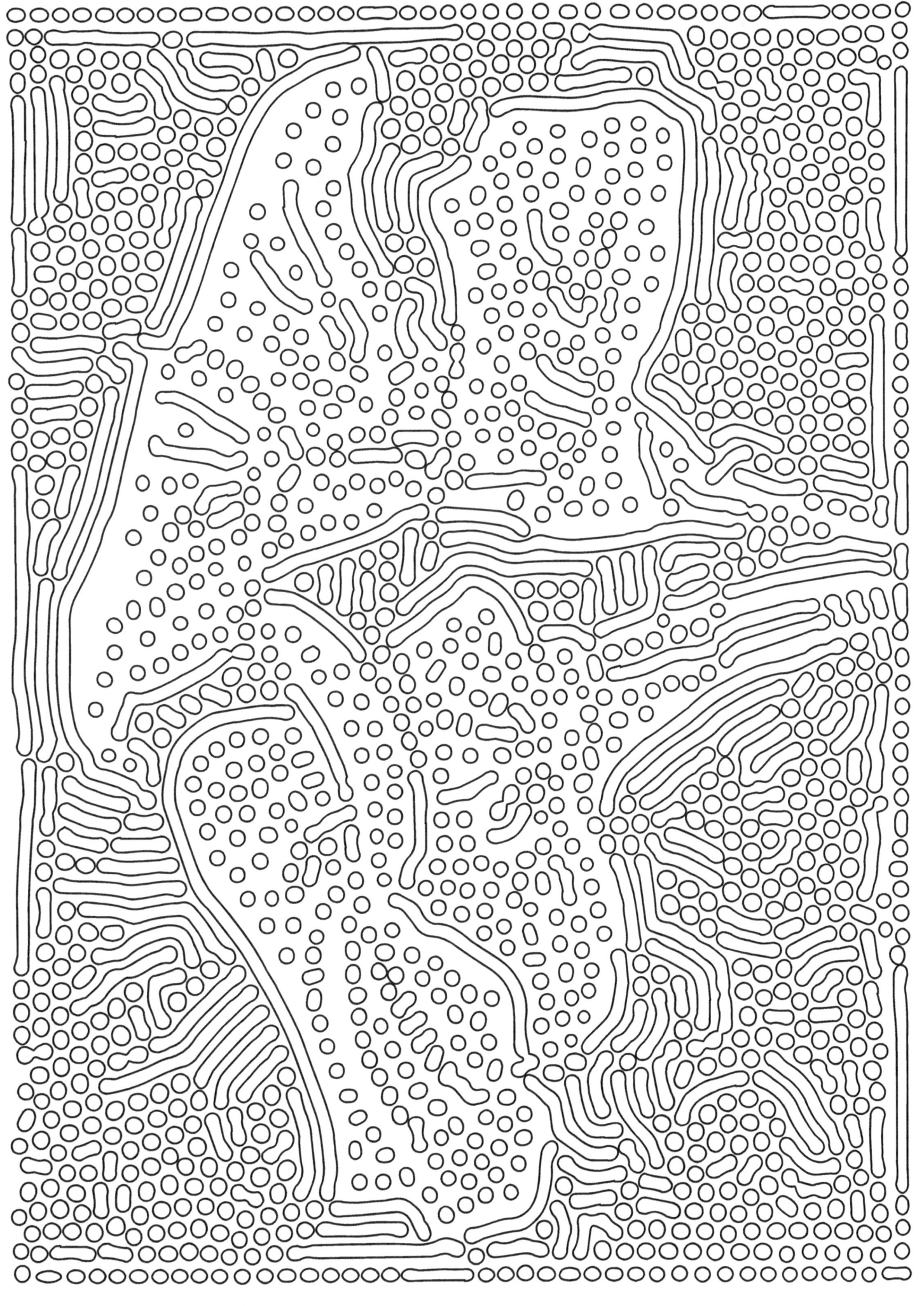

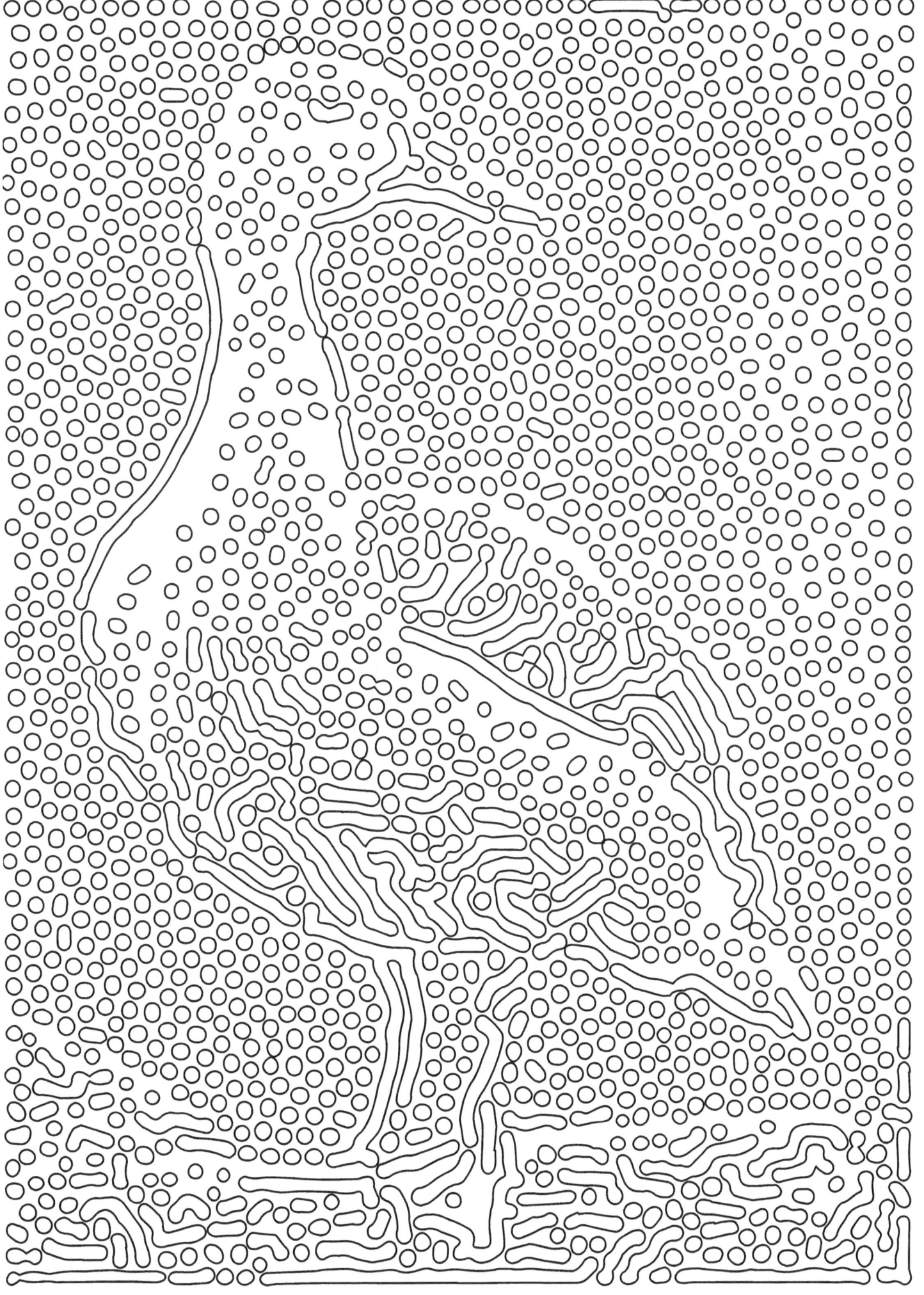

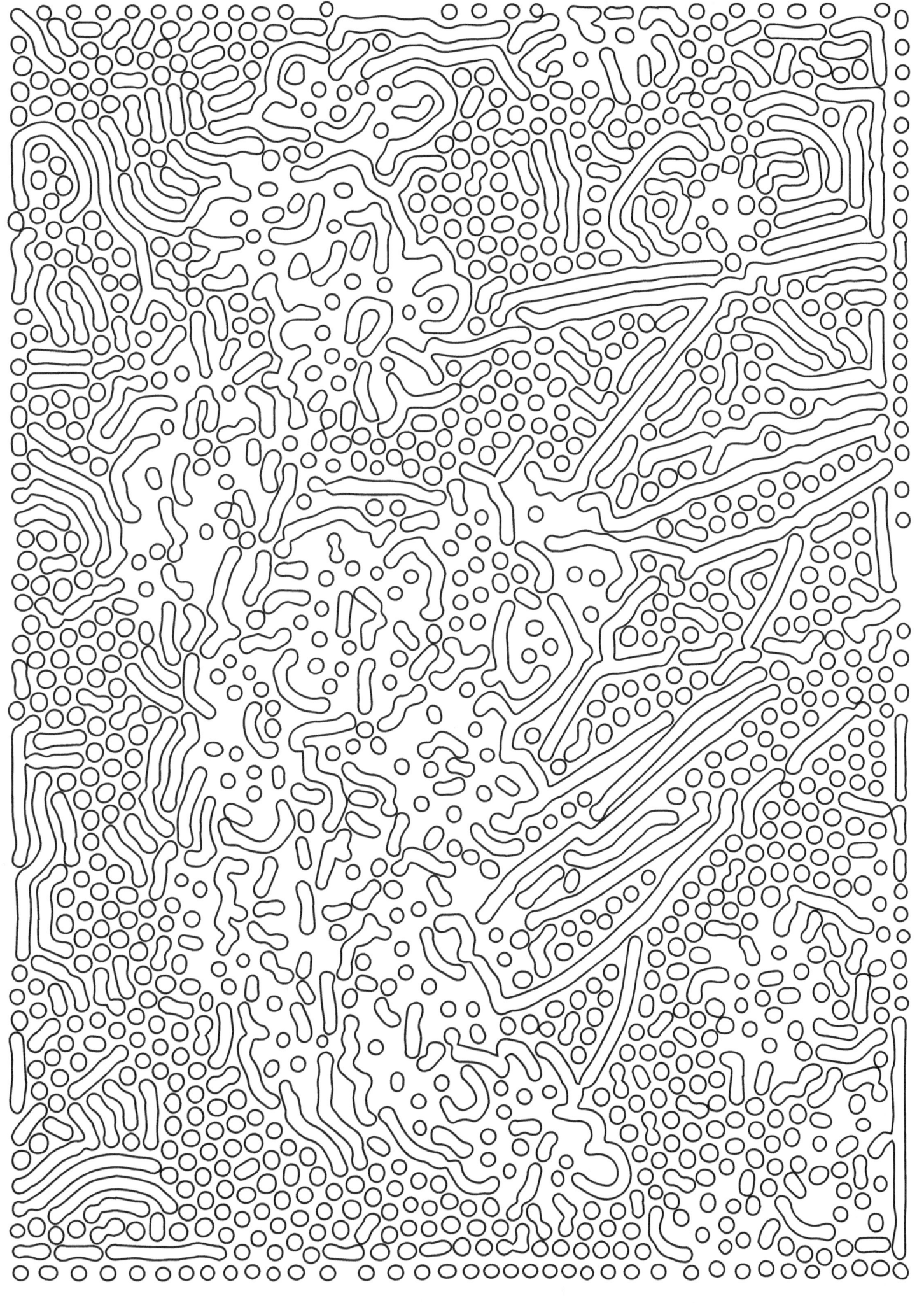

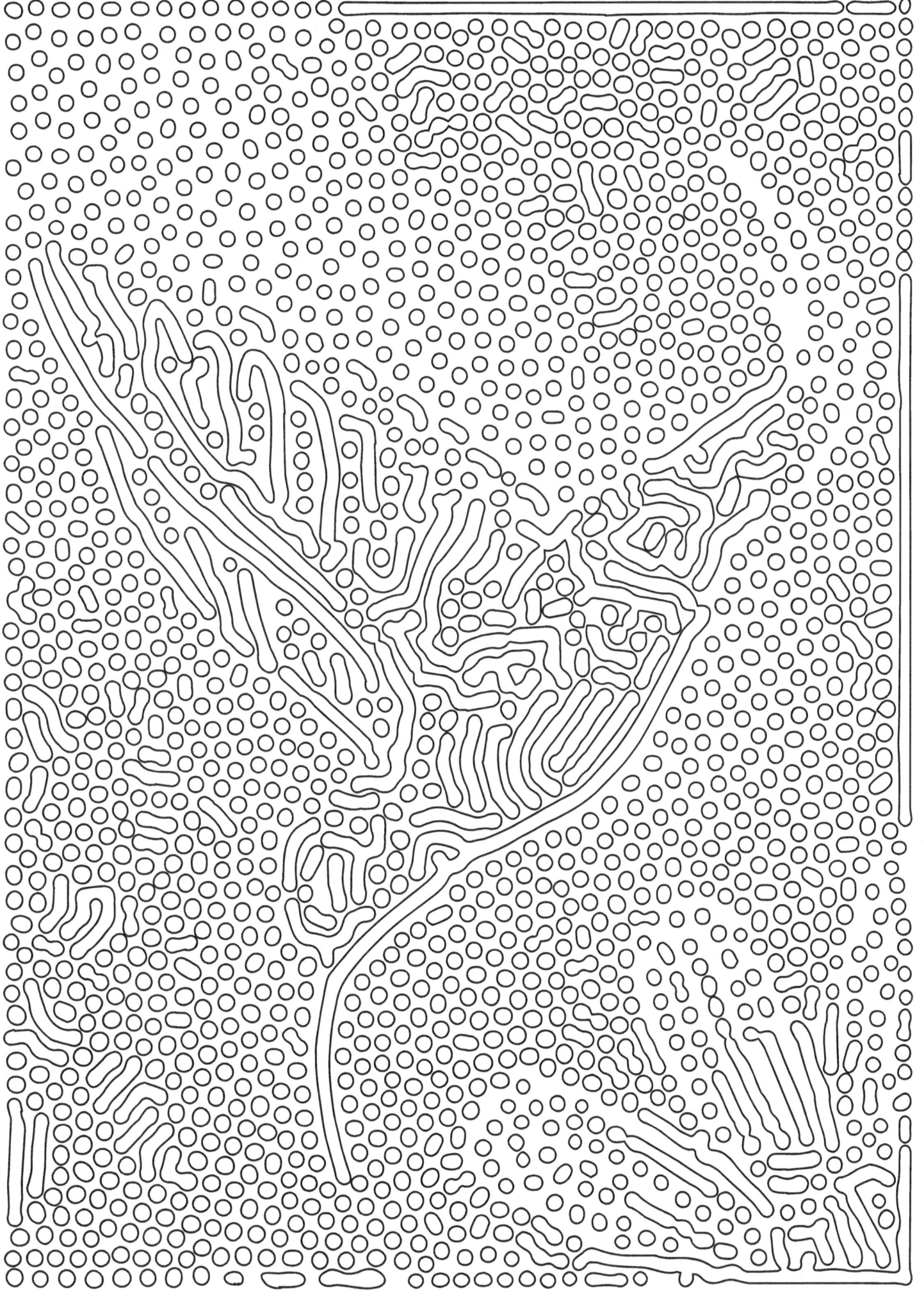

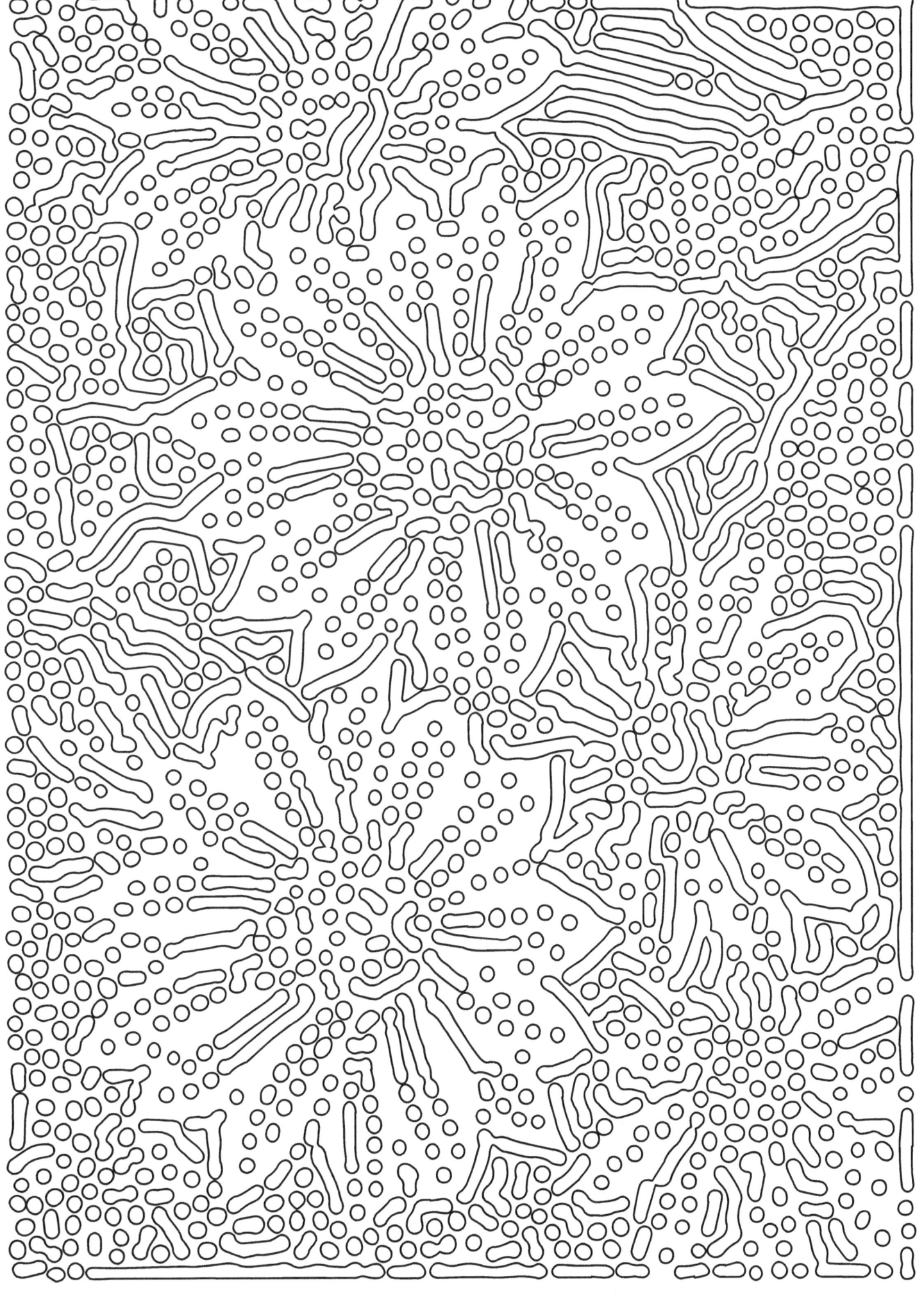

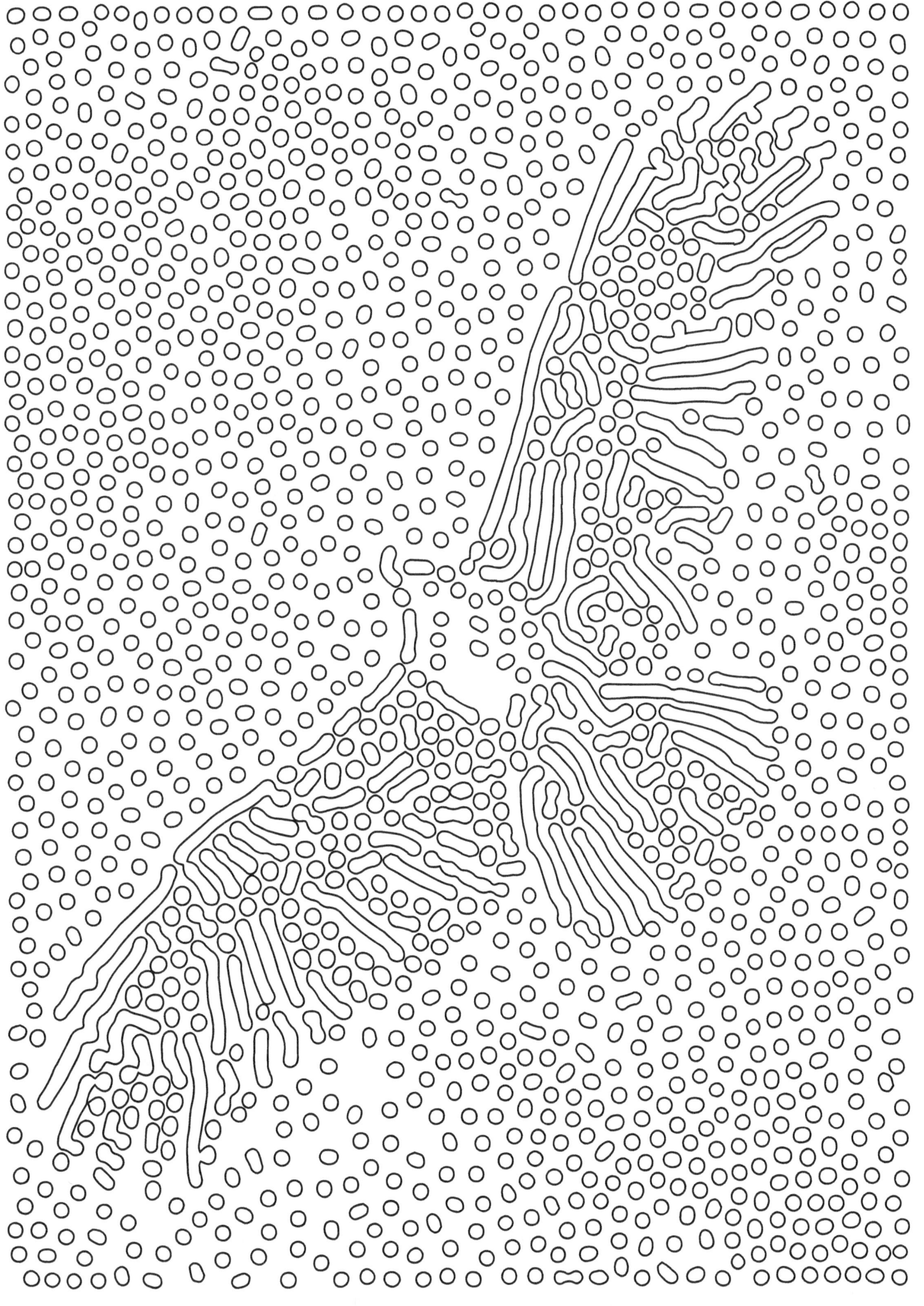

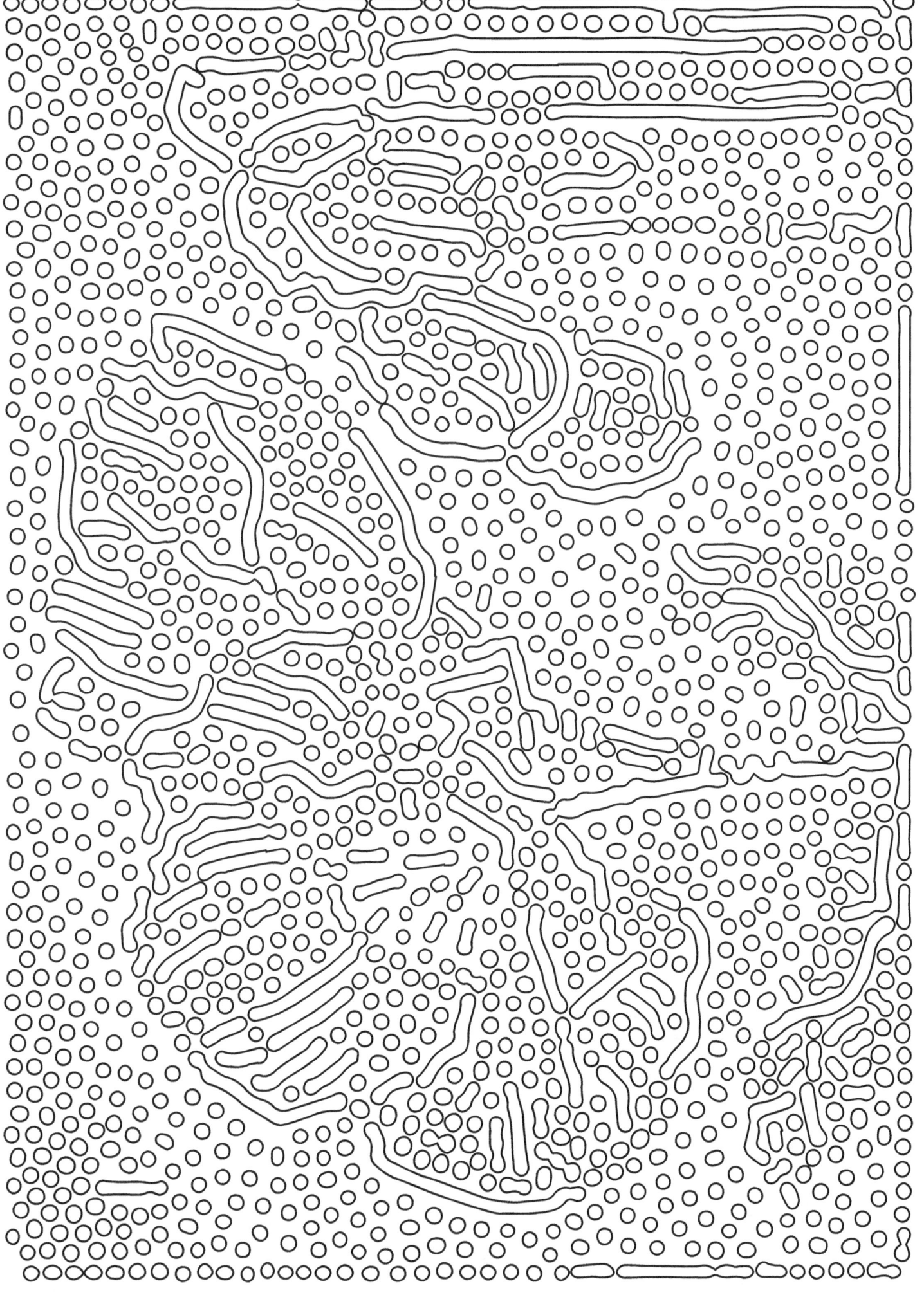

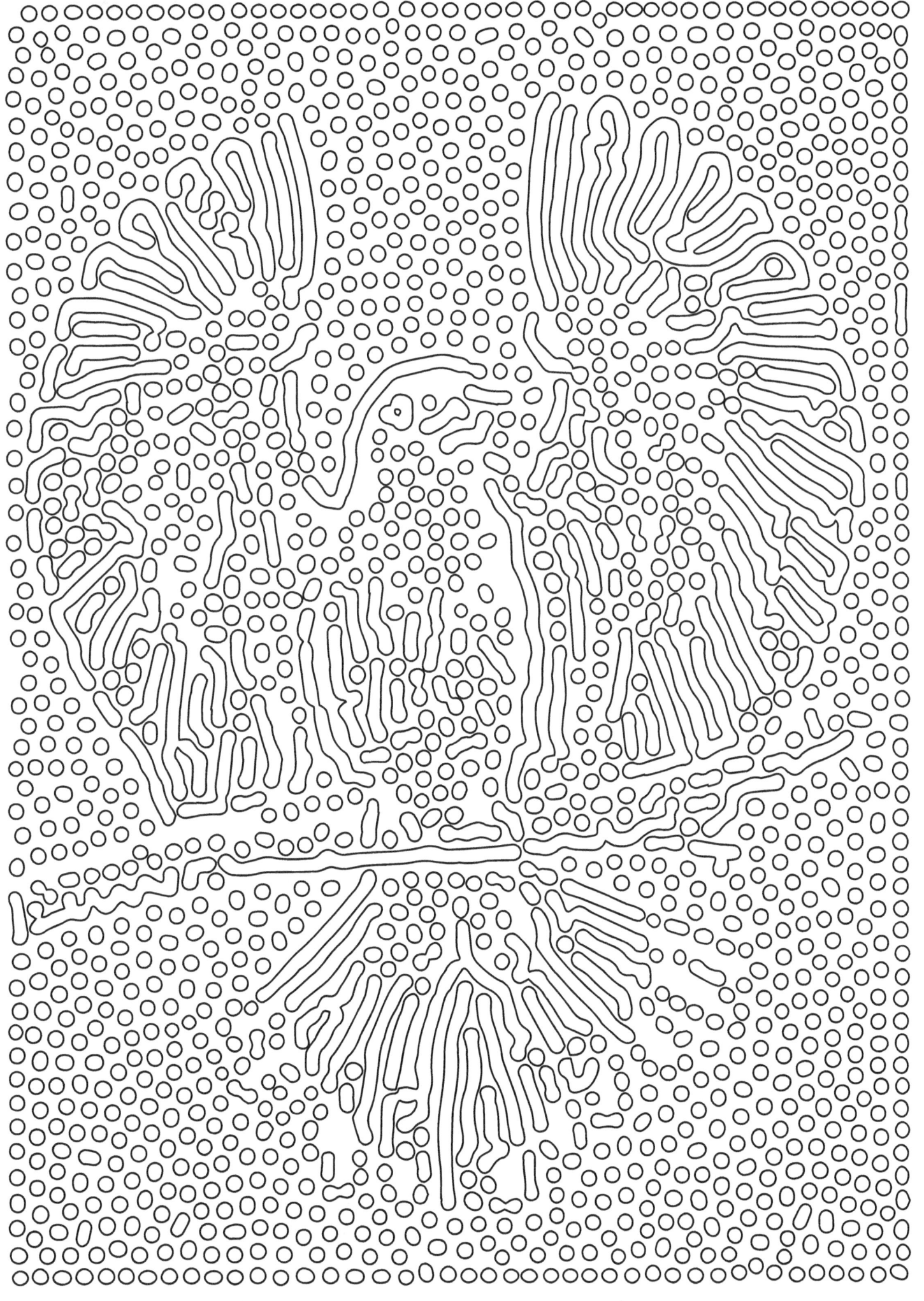

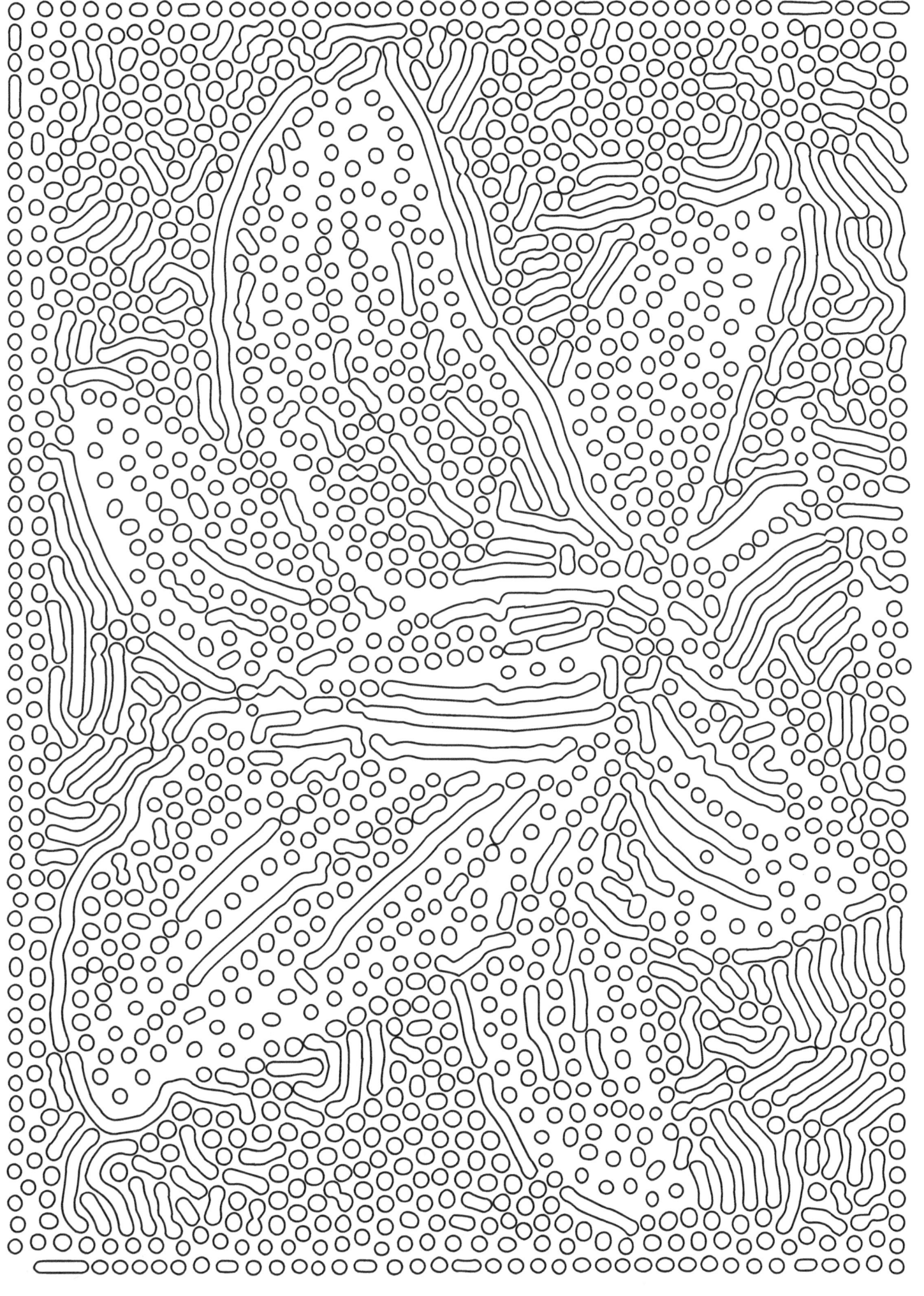

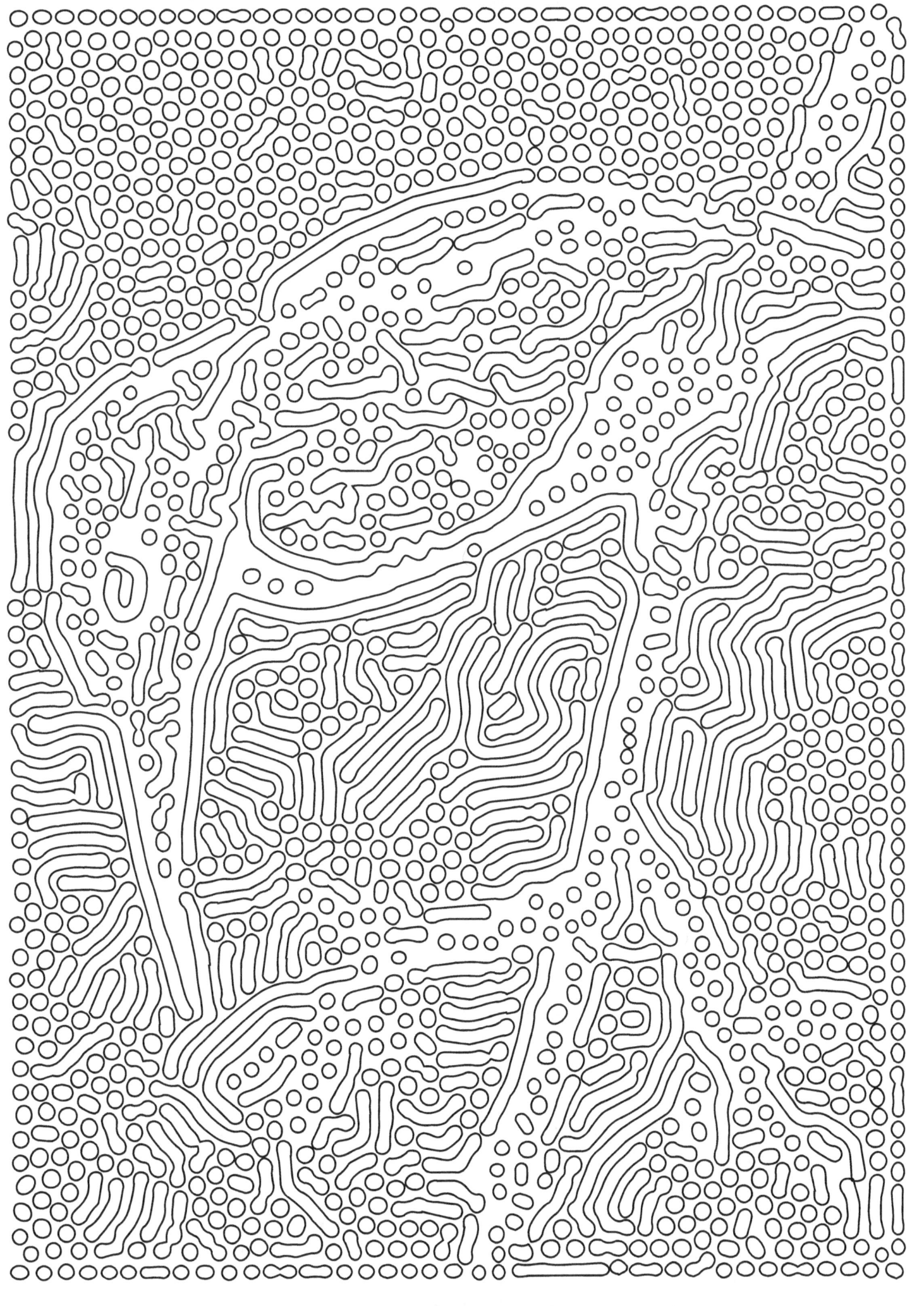

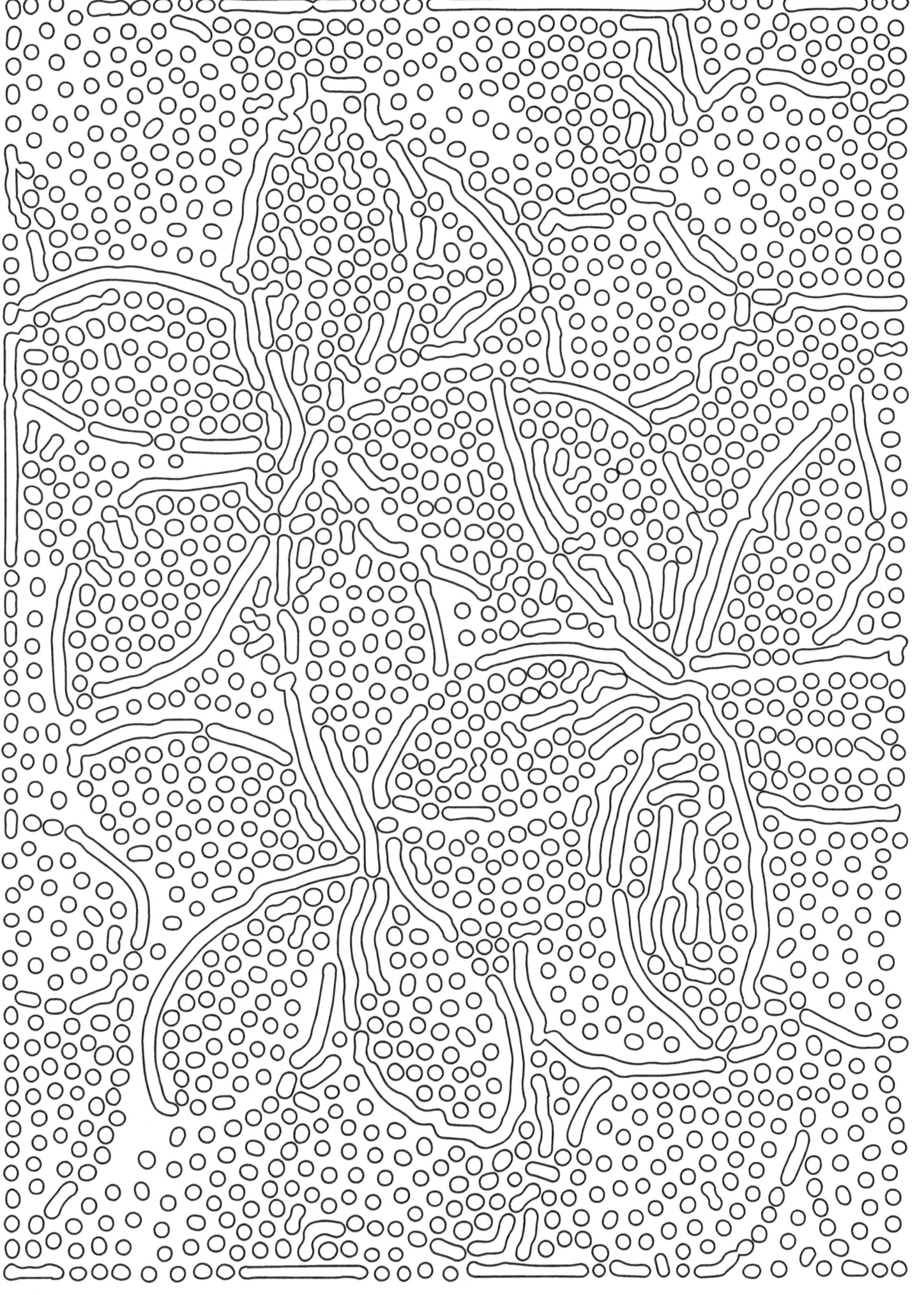

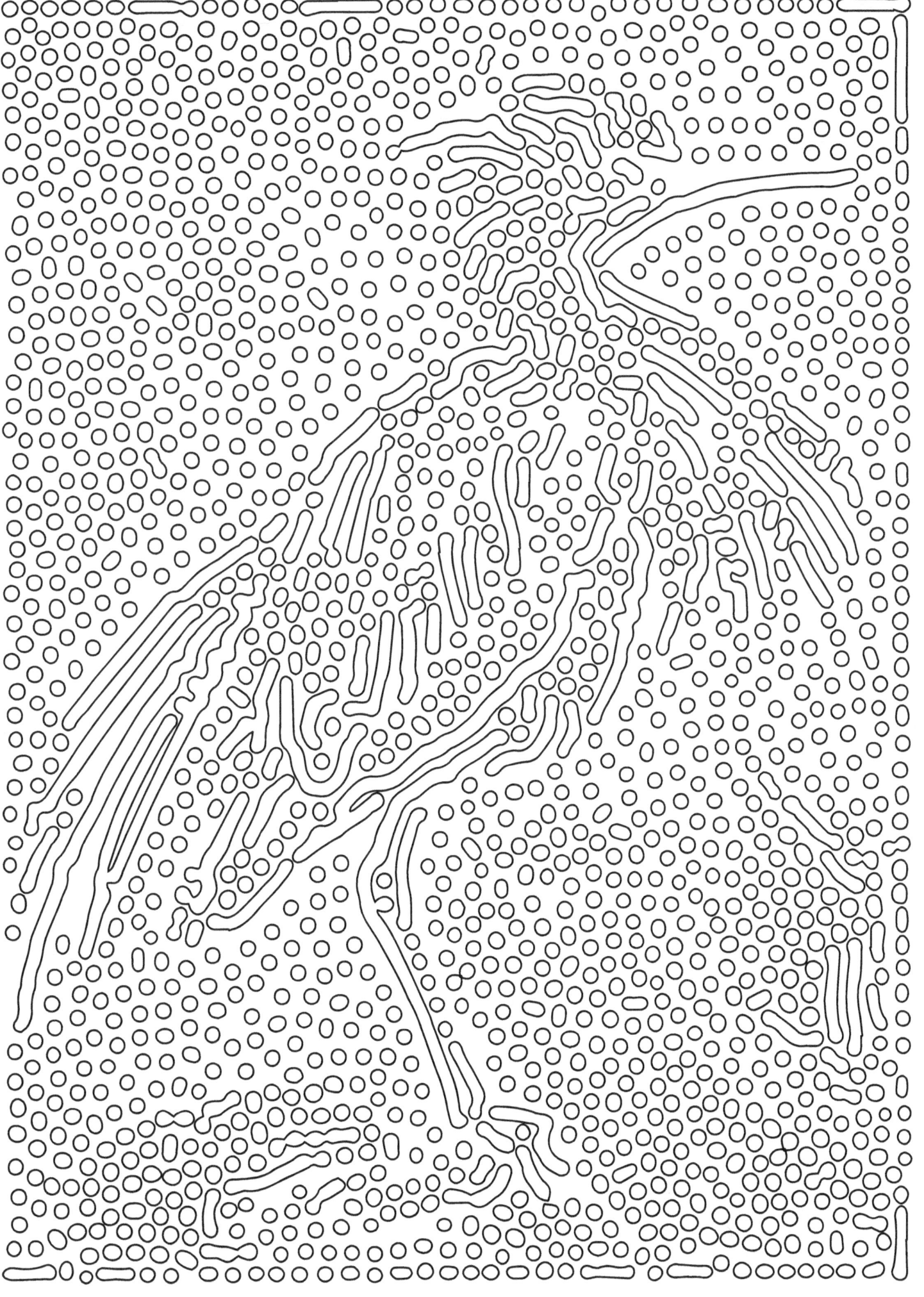

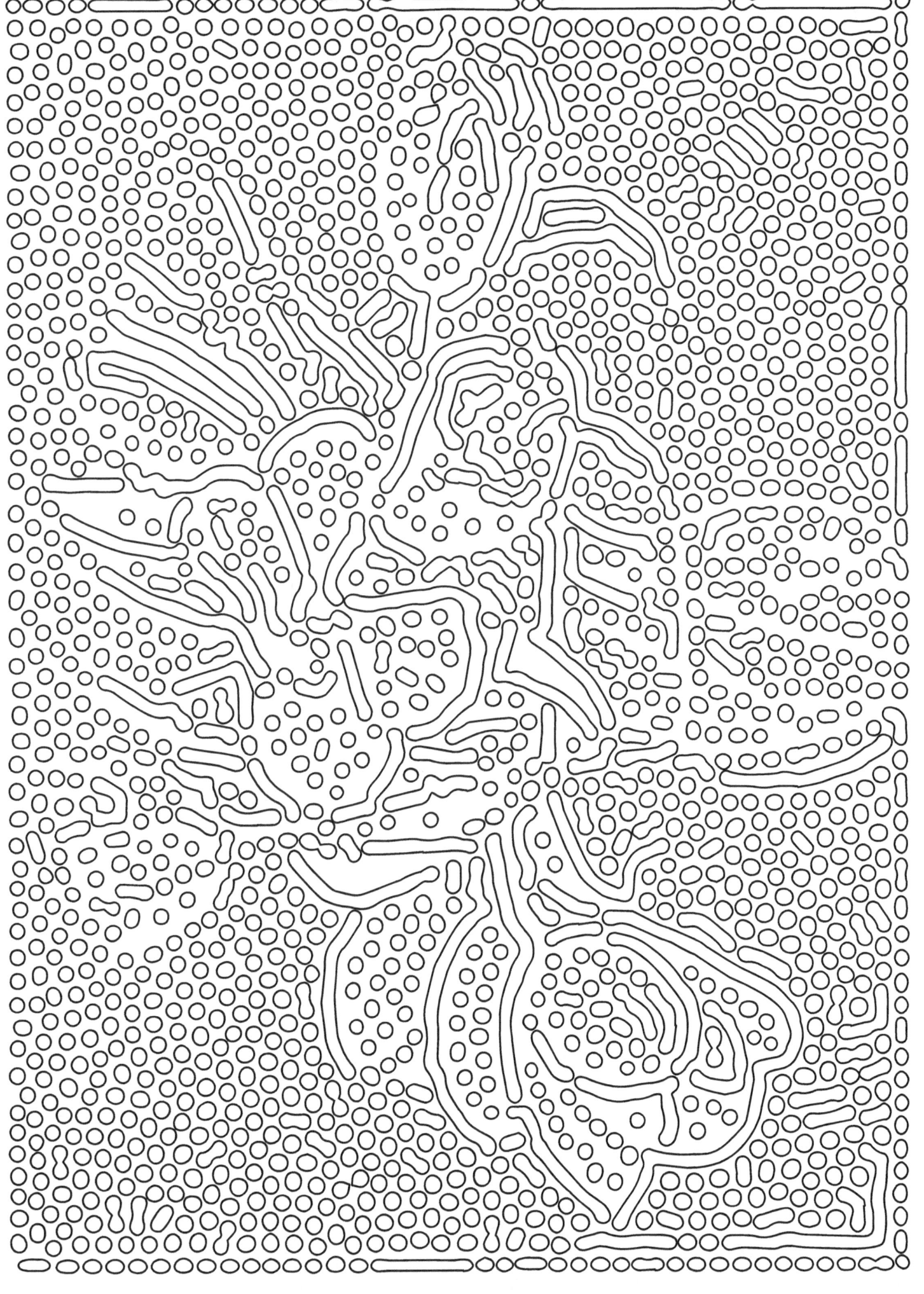

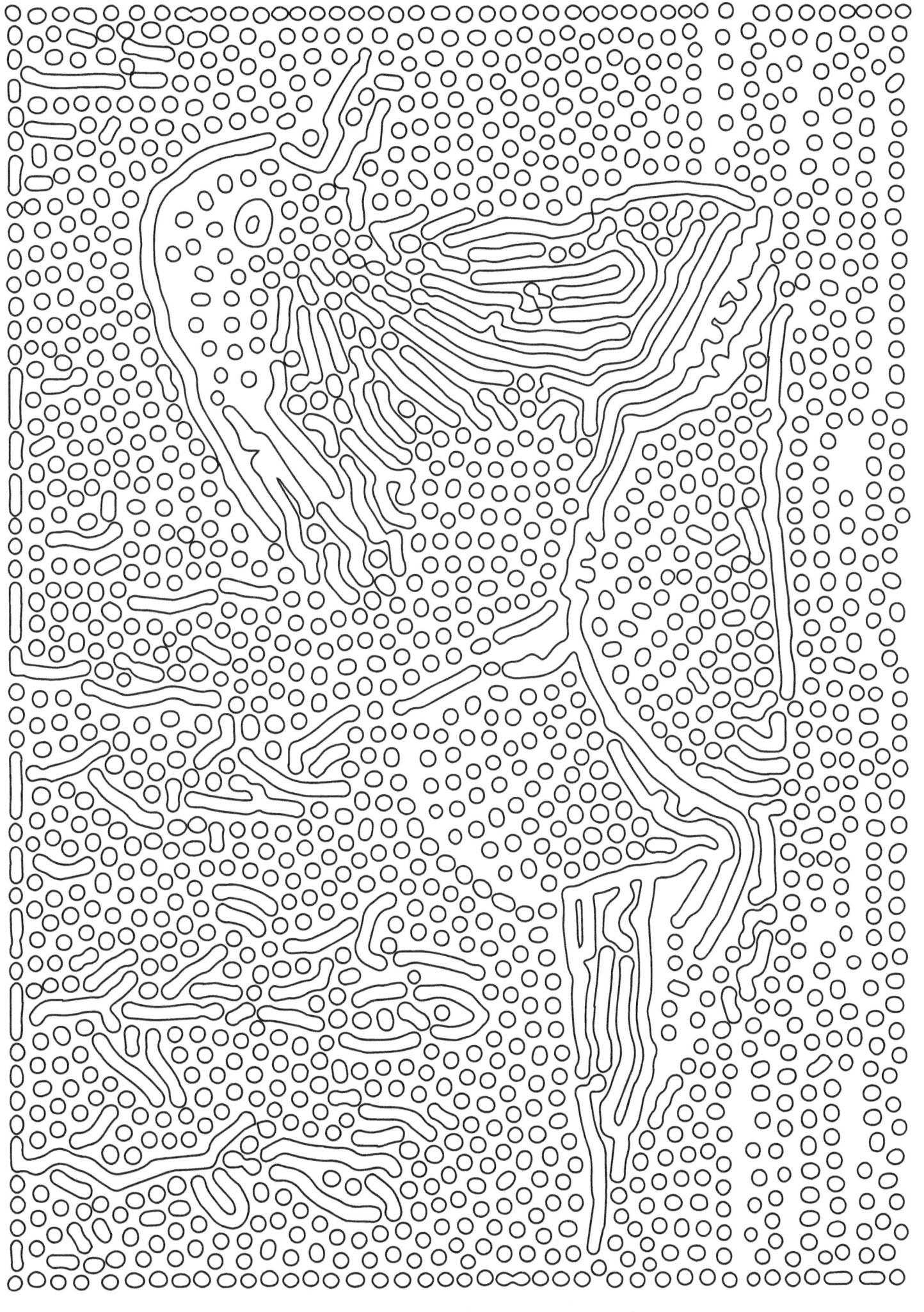

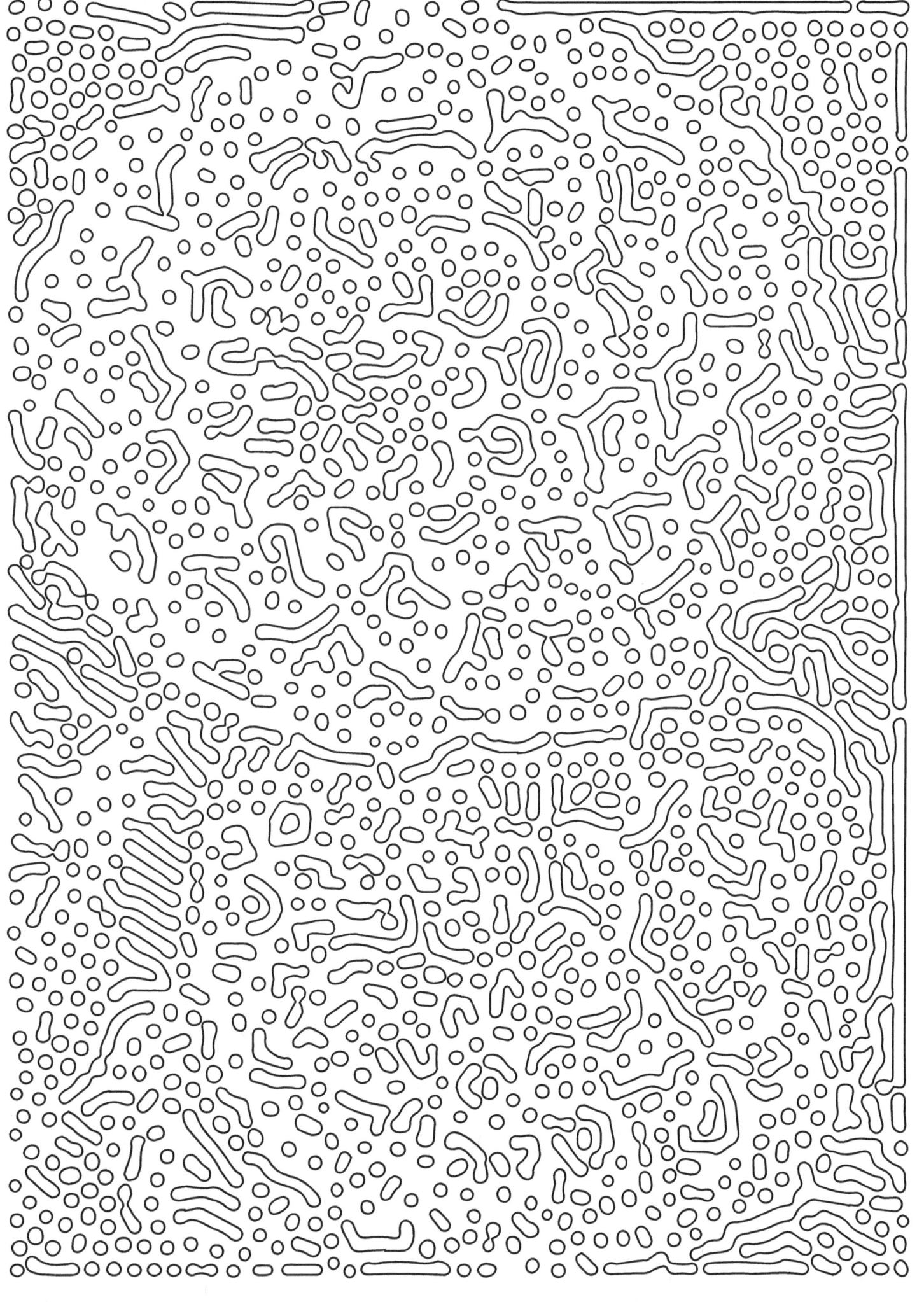